Why Are You Afraid?

Sharing in the Joy of God and His Power Over Evil

Deacon Douglas P. McManaman

DPM Publishing
Aurora, Ontario
2019

DPM also publishes its books in a variety of electronic
formats.

Library and Archives Canada Cataloguing in Publication

McManaman, Douglas
Why Are You Afraid? Sharing in the Joy of God and in His
Power Over Evil
Aurora, Ontario: DPM Publishing. 2010

ISBN: 978-0-9948233-7-3

Cover by Jennifer Johnson, 2019

All Scripture citations are taken from the New American
Bible, USCCB (www.usccb.org)

For Father Lindsay Harrison, whose quiet love of knowledge and dedication to truth helps move the world forward in invisible ways.

Table of Contents

Readings: First Sunday of Lent

First Reading DT 26:4-10

Moses spoke to the people, saying:
"The priest shall receive the basket from you
and shall set it in front of the altar of the Lord, your God.
Then you shall declare before the Lord, your God,
'My father was a wandering Aramean
who went down to Egypt with a small household
and lived there as an alien.
But there he became a nation
great, strong, and numerous.
When the Egyptians maltreated and oppressed us,
imposing hard labor upon us,
we cried to the Lord, the God of our fathers,
and he heard our cry
and saw our affliction, our toil, and our oppression.
He brought us out of Egypt
with his strong hand and outstretched arm,
with terrifying power, with signs and wonders;
and bringing us into this country,
he gave us this land flowing with milk and honey.
Therefore, I have now brought you the firstfruits
of the products of the soil
which you, O Lord, have given me.'
And having set them before the Lord, your God,
you shall bow down in his presence."

Gospel LK 4:1-13

Filled with the Holy Spirit, Jesus returned from the Jordan
and was led by the Spirit into the desert for forty days, to be
tempted by the devil. He ate nothing during those days, and when
they were over he was hungry.
The devil said to him, "If you are the Son of God,
command this stone to become bread."
Jesus answered him, "It is written, One does not live on bread
alone."
Then he took him up and showed him
all the kingdoms of the world in a single instant.
The devil said to him, "I shall give to you all this power and
glory; for it has been handed over to me, and I may give it to
whomever I wish. All this will be yours, if you worship me."
Jesus said to him in reply, "It is written: You shall worship the
Lord, your God, and him alone shall you serve."
Then he led him to Jerusalem, made him stand on the parapet of
the temple, and said to him, "If you are the Son of God, throw
yourself down from here, for it is written: He will command his
angels concerning you, to guard you, and: With their hands they
will support you,
lest you dash your foot against a stone."
Jesus said to him in reply, "It also says, You shall not put the
Lord, your God, to the test."
When the devil had finished every temptation, he departed from
him for a time.

Introduction

In the first reading, Moses summarizes the Jewish story, beginning with Abraham, a wandering Aramean, who went down to Egypt and lived there as an alien. He became a great nation, mighty and populous. And when the Egyptians treated them harshly and afflicted them, imposing hard labor, they cried out to the Lord, the God of our fathers; and the Lord heard their voice and saw their affliction, their toil and oppression. And he delivered them from Egyptian slavery. Their response to this deliverance was worship: He said:

> *So now I bring the first of the fruit of the ground that you, O Lord, have given me. You shall set it down before the Lord your God and bow down before the Lord your God.*

This was better than Cain's offering, who offered not the first fruits of his harvest, but *some* of his harvest. Moses offers the first of the fruit of the ground. God is finally given first place. A nation, namely Israel, in the person of Moses, gives God first place. Abel offered the first born of his flock, but of course Cain killed

Abel, and so at that point the world waits for the offering of Abel to be replaced, and of course Jesus will be the one who replaces Abel's offering of a first-born lamb. That is the fundamental truth about man. In fact, it is the fundamental truth about all of creation. Man's fundamental purpose, his highest activity, is the worship of God. Everything comes from God, but everything exists for God. We live up to our fullest identity when we offer ourselves completely and utterly to God.

And this takes us to our gospel. Jesus was led into the wilderness, like Israel, and for 40 days was tempted by the devil. Jesus' individual life mirrors Israel. But Christ's life is the only life that is pleasing to God, because it is, in its entirely, a perfect offering to God. And that's what human existence is intended to be: a religious offering. And the only way our life can become pleasing to God is by being inserted into the life of the Son of God. He became man so that we can become divinized; God became man so that we can become fully what it means to be a man, a human being, created in the image and likeness of God and called to be a vessel of God.

Unlike Jesus, man failed his first test, a test centered around the tree of the knowledge of good and evil. The symbolism of the tree is profoundly interesting; for a tree is sturdy, independent, self-sufficient, and towering. Furthermore, this tree is called the tree of the "knowledge of good and evil", and children do not know the difference between good and evil; rather, they have to be taught by those who do, and since adults understand, it is adults who are charged with teaching children the difference. Moreover, adulthood is characterized by independence, while childhood is characterized by dependence. This tree symbolizes the desire for independence from God, the desire to be self-sufficient—the temptation is to reject our status as children dependent upon God, and so the sin of the first parents of the human race was the sin of choosing independence from God; it was a rejection of their human status as "child" utterly dependent upon God, who is the measure of what is true and good. It was a decision in favor of the sophistication of adulthood, as opposed to the unsophistication of childhood. Man chose to ignore the limitations of his own nature and to live under the delusion of being more than what he is. The result of such a decision was disaster, a broken world characterized by division, oppression, war, cruelty, hatred, rivalry, fear, death, lovelessness, murder, jealousy, pride, alienation and darkness. And all of it proceeds from the refusal to recognize our limitations, a refusal of our status as dependent children.

In today's gospel, Jesus accomplishes what the first parents of the human race were unable to accomplish, and in doing so, he now renders each one of us capable of rising above sin and temptation so as to achieve our salvation. This really is rooted in the mystery of inheritance. We inherit dispositions from our ancestors. Because they made certain choices in the past, which led to the acquisition of certain habits, we too are now able to begin where they left off, especially if those were good choices. Because someone in our ancestry achieved a certain level of musical and artistic perfection, music became much easier to some of us. And because Christ, the Word made flesh, defeated the evil one and rose above these three specific temptations, every member of the human race is now capable of rising above these very specific temptations, the sins of which have brought ruin to the human race: the temptation to live for the goods of this world, the temptation to sell your soul for the glory of power, achievement, and success, and finally the temptation to doubt the word of God and to put God to the test. And when we achieve a certain level of perfection in the spiritual life, we influence others we don't necessarily even know personally, who may not even be in our immediate vicinity, who may not even exist right now, but will next year or the year after, etc. It is very mysterious how this works, but there is so much about the nature of reality that we know virtually nothing about.

There is tremendous evil in the world, much of it hidden, and it is all rooted in the three different concupiscences: of the flesh, of the eyes, and the pride of life. And life in Christ is a battle precisely because his life was a battle, a war, and there will always be, until the end of time, two opposing sides who are at war. The one side is characterized by the rejection of man's status as child dependent upon God; the other side is characterized by a love and acceptance of that status. And the good news is that we know in advance that this battle has already been won; there is a clear winner and a loser. History is like one great game of chess. The problem for one side is that God cannot lose a game of chess. He is all knowing, and He is supremely good. If your opponent knows from all eternity what move you are going to make, he cannot lose the game. And God knows what move his opponents will make, for God is omniscient, and so God cannot lose this global game of chess.

Every human person has to decide what side he will join. It is, however, important to keep in mind that the winning side always looks as if it is losing—after all, Jesus died on a cross. And the losing side always looks as if it is winning. But the winning side walks by faith, by virtue of the limitations that constrain us. We don't see the entire meaning of things through the natural light of the intellect, but only through revelation and with the mind and heart of Christ. But that mind and heart has to be more fully appropriated every day.

For the rest of this book, I want to unpack some of the details of this historical and global battle from the perspective of the gospel. I want to focus on how Christ was able to defeat the one enemy that we could not defeat, namely sin and death, and I want to focus on how we participate in that battle and share in the glory of his victory, and how we share in the influence he has on this world.

The Bread of Life

This morning's gospel was about the temptation in the wilderness. I'd like to take this time to draw out a few points on the basis of the first two temptations. I am going to suggest that Jesus underwent these temptations for one reason only—so that we would be given the capacity to rise above those temptations in our own life; our life is a participation in his victory over evil. It is only because he defeated the evil one that we can defeat him in our own lives, and, when we do so in our own lives, we also make it possible for others after us to rise above sin in order to choose God.

I teach at a Catholic high school in Markham, and because it is an IB World school, we tend to get bright and hardworking students. But there was something about the students this year; they are very good, very smart, but I felt something was missing in one of the classes I had. I don't want to say that they were dead; their minds were very much alive, but I sensed that they were a bit too focused on their goals—and they had very lofty goals. I sensed that the very center of their lives was their own personal achievement, and so I asked them: "You have two alternatives before you. It is up to you to choose your path. On the first path is a six-figure salary, a great job, travel, lots of leisure, eating in the finest restaurants, a long life of pleasure and excitement, the only problem is you have to put your conscience in the freezer. You have to be willing to do things, such as lying, fraud, etc., but a long and exciting life is yours. That's the first option. The second option: minimum wage, you are mopping floors, living in a dingy apartment in Scarborough, can't afford to travel nor eat in the finest restaurants, but you have a good conscience, you have not sold your soul. How many of you would take the first road, the six-figure salary and all, but with your conscience in a deep freeze?" All of them except one put up their hands; virtually all of them would put their conscience in the freezer for the sake of an opulent life here. The one student who chose to mop floors for minimum wage is in the chapel every morning.

As you know, the devil said to him, "If you are the Son of God, command this stone to become bread." And Jesus replies: "Man does not live by bread alone, but by every word that comes from the mouth of

God". These are words from the Old Testament (Dt 8,3), and Jesus uses these words to defeat the evil one in the first temptation in the desert. The word of God is a powerful weapon. To read the word of God every day, to pray the Scriptures every day, is to be empowered by that word. And when our life is rooted in that word, it is rooted in the Truth, and when our life is rooted in the Truth, we are less easily deceived. We become more intuitive, much more aware of the will of God in our lives, and we become a very difficult project for the devil to defeat.

What Christ says here is that our life is not bread; our life, the life that Christ speaks of when he says that man does not live by bread alone, does not consist in the goods of this world. The pleasures of this world are temporary; they pass away, but our life is not meant to pass away. We were created for eternity, and bread cannot sustain us for very long. Jesus said: "I have come that you may have life and have it abundantly" (Jn 10, 10). The pleasures of this world are good, but they are not the abundant life he is speaking of. Rather, the Word that proceeds from God the Father is our life. In him do we find a life rich in mystery and meaning, a life of never-ending surprises.

The students I mention above are really wonderful students, they come from good families, but for many of them, the very center of their lives is a bread that will pass away, a bread that does not give life. Only one student, the one who is able to discern the bread of life in an ordinary chapel, is willing to mop floors for minimum wage and live in a dingy apartment, barely making ends meet, because she has experienced the joy that comes from above, as well as the pleasures that come from the earth, and she knows that there's no comparison.

Bread, of course, can stand for food, or it can represent money, the means to purchase whatever we need to sustain our life. In fact, in the 70s, 'bread' was slang for money. The fundamental temptation that plagues everybody in this life is to look upon and treat everything that is a means to sustaining our life, such as food, drink, money, shelter, etc., as if it were our very life. Food comes from below us, from the ground, and so too money, at least money in the sense of sound currency, such as gold or silver—not the fiat currency created out of thin air by the central banks. Bread and everything it represents is below our life; literally comes from the ground.

But although we came from the ground (humus), we were not created *for* the ground, for what is below us, but rather for what is above us. The bread that is below us is necessary, of course, but it exists to serve a higher good—the Bread of Life, which is the Word that proceeds from the Father. Without that sustenance, the goods of this world really become empty promises. They can't deliver. The pleasures and goods of this world are exhaustible; they run out, they get old. It is very hard to get people to see this if they have not experienced this before. Think of Christ's first miracle at the wedding at Cana; the wine ran out. What does Jesus do? He tells the servants: fill the six stone water jars, which held the water for the Jewish rites of purification, used to wash peoples' feet, considered to be the lowest of tasks, reserved for the servants. The thought of drinking anything from those stone jars would have been thoroughly disgusting for anyone at the time. Jesus turns this water, contained and contaminated by these dirty vessels, into a wine better than the wine served at the beginning of the wedding. And six hundred litres of this wine. My gas tank holds 40 litres. That would be the equivalent of 15 tanks of wine. It takes me more than 3 months to go through 15 tanks of gasoline. That's an overabundance of wine. The result would have been one cheerful party.

The wine is a symbol of the joy that Christ came to bring. The problem is that most people confuse pleasure with joy. Thomas Merton once said: "Never seek rest in pleasure, for you were not created for pleasure, you were created for joy; and if you do not know the difference between pleasure and joy, you have not yet begun to live". Most people today have not begun to live; for they have no idea what the difference is between pleasure and joy. They've experienced great pleasures in their lives, but not joy. The difference between the two can perhaps be compared to the difference between water and wine. Water is pleasant when you are thirsty, but wine is altogether different, as you well know.

But this scene of the wine running out is great symbolism, because the pleasures of this world run out; everything in this world eventually gets old. And the reason is that we were not created for this world, we are only passing through this life. We were created for the joy of knowing God as He is in Himself, and this life is a preparation for that. As Paul says in Colossians:

> *He is the image of the invisible God,*
> *the first-born of all creatures.*
> *In him everything in heaven and on earth was created,*
> *things visible and invisible.*
> *All were created through him;*
> *all were created for him.*

We were created *for* Christ, the Word made flesh.

I often enjoy watching *Dragon's Den*; these people know a great deal about the business world, they are very smart people obviously, and they are tremendously wealthy—hopefully through honest and legitimate means, but they have never come across to me as joyful; content, yes, but not joyful; no doubt enjoying a life of travel and great pleasures and excitements, things that money can buy. But a joyful person is something else entirely. I have met joyful people before, people who have much less money, much less leisure time, less pleasures in their lives, but they radiate joy. They know the Lord. They are at rest. There is a joy they know that is impossible to describe to those who have never tasted it, sort of like trying to describe the experience of being somewhat drunk on good wine to someone who has never tasted wine, only water. Interestingly enough, on Pentecost—when the Holy Spirit descended upon the Apostles—some of those who witnessed the effects of this descent of the Holy Spirit thought the Apostles were drunk: "They have been drinking too much new wine", they said. The new wine is a symbol of the joy that is one of the fruits of the Holy Spirit.

Christ said I have come that you may have life, and have it abundantly, overflowing in abundance, sort of like 600 litres of wine at a wedding. The wine of this world runs out, it gets old, it loses its potency, but Christ brings a new wine.

I've always wanted to go to Ireland and see the rich green landscape, visit the pubs, see the ocean, thatched cottages, etc., but one day I was at the Toronto Pearson Airport waiting to pick up someone in the winter. I overhear this Irish couple who had just flown in from Ireland to visit Toronto, Canada for a vacation. Why in the world would you want to visit Toronto in the winter when you got Ireland? And, of course, the answer is that the goods of this world can only bring us so much, and nothing more, and so we continue to search as if another geographic location in this world is going to do the trick. But we were created for more than what this world can deliver

There's got to be something more to life than this, and of course there is, and it is precisely this that injects a different kind of life into the goods of this world. Without that life from above, that comes from God, this life eventually becomes wretched, like the water in the stone jars, and it is always ultimately empty. But with that life given from above, the simplest goods of this world take on a life that is inexhaustible. By itself, the bread of this world can only give so much, but when that bread has become part of a life that is given from above, a life overflowing with divine grace, then it acquires the meaning it was originally intended to have. Just like the Eucharist—it was bread, but now, although it looks like nothing more than a mere wafer of bread, it contains the body, blood, soul and divinity of Christ, who is our life and origin. My spiritual director is in his 80s now, and for his birthdays over the past few years he was given money in order to travel, to get out of Toronto, and visit Ireland, Spain, Italy, etc. But he told me that it's all just sitting there, he hasn't touched it, he doesn't feel the need to, because he knows that when he gets to these places, he's just going to visit the Basilicas and the Cathedrals and spend time before the Blessed Sacrament, and he said to me: "I have the Blessed Sacrament here in the chapel. I can just go there; I don't have to fly across the ocean to visit the Blessed Sacrament."

Some of us might know from within just what he means; he has travelled before, and he knows through experience that what he can get over there that he cannot get over here eventually gets old, you've seen it all before, but what really gives life and inexhaustible meaning to these mundane experiences is something that we have access to wherever there is a Church with the Blessed Sacrament, and that is the Life that Christ is; and he knows that that is the origin of an enduring joy, a joy that does not pass away.

Jesus' individual life is parallel to the life of Israel, God's covenanted people, who spent 40 years in the Desert before entering the land of Canaan. Our individual life is in many ways a life in the desert, because it is a preparation for eternal life. And any kind of preparation involves suffering, setbacks, difficulties, labor. Our life here in this world is a life in the wilderness, for it involves suffering and frustrations. And the reason this is fitting is that *human beings are at their worst in times of prosperity, but we are at our best in times of suffering.* I remember that this point was brought home to me once again in 2008 when I was ordained and asked to visit a patient in a psychiatric institution. Why does God allow so much suffering in this world? I've been asking that question since I was a teenager, and over time my understanding of that question continues to deepen. There's no way for me to properly answer that question when it comes to the life of an individual person; I have no idea why God has permitted this or that suffering or tragedy to enter into the life of a particular person, and it would be Olympian arrogance for me to attempt an answer; to do so as it relates to a particular person requires a knowledge of details that we just don't have, a knowledge of this person's past, present, and future, as well as a knowledge of the mind of God and the plan of providence, and all this is outside our range. We just don't know, and it is not for us to know.

But we do know this on a general level, namely, that God is goodness itself, the source of all that is good; God is absolute love. He wills our greatest good, our greatest happiness. Furthermore, He is all powerful, which means He can bring about our greatest happiness, our greatest good. He wants the best for us, and He has the power to bring it about, unlike us who are parents; for although we want the best for our children, we simply don't have the power to bring it about. But God is both omnipotent and Supremely Good. He wills the best for us, our greatest happiness, and He has the power to make it happen. Hence, it follows that whatever God permits to happen in our lives, He allows it for our greatest happiness, our greatest good. We know this, because if something happened to us, God permitted it. And we also know He loves us, and if we knew how much God loves each of us individually, here and now, we would die of joy. I believe it was St. Catherine of Siena who said that God loves each one of us as if there is only one of us—as if you are the only one to love. He permitted this and that to happen, and He could have prevented it, because He's all powerful, and at the same time He wills my greatest happiness, that I live in joy. Beyond that, we can't say much about an individual person's situation. Human suffering is very mysterious.

But I was asked to visit a particular patient who suffered from paranoid schizophrenia. I've had a number of patients with paranoid schizophrenia over the years, and it's a horrible illness. But this one person that I saw regularly began, after a while, to tell me about his life before the illness. When he did so, I remember thinking to myself that this illness is a real blessing for him, a gift, because if this person had never come down with this particular mental illness, he would have been a lost soul for sure. He was very far down the road of moral depravity, the details of which I will leave out, and something happened in his life that triggered the illness, a stressor, one that he was likely the cause of, and now he has to live every day with the thought that there is a large group of people watching him always, ready to catch him doing something wrong. I say his illness was a real blessing, because now he prays, he is very devout, and there are moments when he experiences great joy in his prayer life. He lives for the Eucharist, he lives for Christ. But his devotion and relationship to God began only after he began sinking into the water, like Peter, who reached out and called out to the Lord to help him. That probably would not have happened without his illness.

We are at our worst in times of prosperity, but we are at our best in times of suffering. This is certainly true in the history of Israel. If you follow the Old Testament, during times of prosperity and blessing, Israel begins to fall away from fidelity to the covenant, and then she enters a period of suffering, and she is overpowered by her enemies. And then she returns to a faithful observance of the Torah in a spirit of repentance and blessing eventually returns. This is true in the history of North America as well. As a result of Original Sin, we have a real tendency or inclination to selfishness, to self-seeking. The first wound of Original Sin is the concupiscence of the flesh, which is a disordered love of physical gratification. And this wound brings about a disordered love of self. Think of any kind of wound, such as a toothache; all we can think about when we have a toothache is ourselves. The direction and focus of our attention is toward the self. We carry that wound of Original Sin; we have a propensity to focus on ourselves. The spiritual life is about dying to that excessive love of self; it is really about gradually shifting the direction of our life away from the self, putting God at the center and the self at the periphery. And the reason is that we are only just passing through this life; we are here for a short time only, and everything, if you notice, is a preparation for the next stage of development: kindergarten is a preparation for elementary school, which in turn is a preparation for high school, which in turn is a preparation for university, which is a preparation for life in the world of work and family. But what is life a preparation for? We were created for an eternal life of union with God, who is Love, and so this life is about learning to love, learning to follow. But to follow we must listen, and listening requires silence, and fasting brings silence to one's interior. And God speaks in the silence of the heart.

In silence, we adopt a posture. It is a listening posture, and our attention is turned outward, away from the self. And it is fasting that brings about that interior silence. St. John of the Cross refers to this as bringing stillness to the house of the soul. When everything within us is still, we can hear God speak. We are sensitive to His inspiration.

It is very difficult to know what it is God wants us to do in our lives; in fact, you could say it is impossible, and so we really should not pray to know what God wants us to do in our lives. Rather, we should pray *to want* to do what God wants us to do. 'Let me want to do what you want me to do, Lord'; and it is when the heart is detached from the goods and pleasures of this world that it is free to be moved in a certain direction by the Holy Spirit. This is reminiscent of Elijah who discovered the Lord in the quiet breeze. God's inspiration is subtle, like a quiet breeze, but we have to be disposed to notice it. If we don't fast, we won't listen, and it will be very easy to take a wrong path, and very easy to convince ourselves that the path we have taken is the right path. We were created for an eternal life of union with God, and that union has to begin here in this life.

Selling One's Soul

And then the devil led him up and showed him in an instant all the kingdoms of the world. 'To you will I give their glory and all this authority; for it has been given over to me, and I give it to anyone I please. If you worship me, it will all be yours.'

Of course, Jesus responds by quoting once again the word of God: "You shall worship the Lord, your God, and him alone shall you serve." This represents Christ's defeat over the concupiscence of the eyes, the original temptation in the garden. In the third chapter of Genesis, the woman saw that the fruit was a delight to the eyes. This refers to inordinate ambition; the disordered desire for independence, for authority over others, the disordered desire for security, for control, in short, a disordered desire for the glory of power. Christ's victory here is a victory over diabolical narcissism.

As a teacher, I often think we do our students a disservice by placing so much emphasis on academic achievement with all our awards ceremonies; ultimately, there is only one thing that is going to matter when this life is over, and that is not going to be a record of how much money we made, or how successful we were in our work, or the number of awards we might have received. The only thing that will matter is whether throughout our lives we have loved. That alone will be your joy at the end of your life; nothing else. Everything else will have gone.

We are here to learn how to love, how to love God and how to love our neighbor. It's very hard for people to love anything other than themselves when they don't believe that there is anything other than this life and the goods of this world to live for. That's when people become anxious and fearful, and they tend to focus primarily on their own survival. And that's when life becomes cold; the world becomes a cold place. A living organism is warm, but a corpse is cold.

I always try to impress upon young people the point that character is everything. We will be judged on our character, and we determine ourselves to be a certain kind of person (character) by the moral choices that we make. You are what you will, said St. Theresa of Lisieux. Even Aristotle said: "You are not what you think, and you are not what you feel, but you are what you will". I remember telling that to a mental health patient I visited once at the hospital. I think he had schizophrenia; he was convinced he was evil, because he couldn't control his thoughts, and those thoughts were disturbing; they were "evil thoughts". He also felt as if he were completely worthless. And I remember telling him that I was just talking about this to my students, and I quoted Aristotle who said you are not what you think, and you are not what you feel, but you are what you will. It was a real epiphany for him; his eyes opened wide with hope. What do you will to be? What are you trying to be? What are you choosing to be? That's who you are. I think it was the only time I got a thank you card from a patient.

When scripture speaks of the heart, it refers to the will. The heart that we shape by the choices that we make will be our eternity. Again, St. John of the Cross refers to the heart as a house. That house is our mansion, our dwelling place, and it will be ours forever. If that heart is cold as a result of the fire of the divine love being extinguished, if our heart becomes a freezer, then our eternal dwelling place will be a freezer. And that will be our hell. But if there is movement, if there is life within the heart, there is warmth, there is heat, there is a burning flame, and that dwelling place won't be a hell, but a heaven; our dwelling place for all eternity.

I've had a lot of practice preaching hell. My first ten years as a teacher were in the Jane and Finch area of Toronto, and they were difficult years. We had some pretty difficult students, and after a while I knew that the only chance I had to get through to some of them was to begin sounding like an Evangelical preacher. When you're dealing with drug dealers or kids who have no problem punching an 80-year-old woman in the head in order to get her purse, sublime theology and philosophical reasoning don't go very far. You have to speak a language they understand, which is a very black and white language, so I learned early on to be very direct and very blunt when dealing with certain kinds of students. I'd walk into what was probably a drug deal taking place in the school washroom; what do you do? You give them a sermon on hell! If that doesn't work, nothing will; so, I got pretty good at scaring the heck out of certain kinds of people.

The students I deal with now, however, are well brought up and they are some of the finest students in the city, so I don't have to use those tactics anymore; they listen to reason. But when students ask about hell, I always recall what my friend the Late Monsignor Tom Wells from the Archdiocese of Washington D. C. used to tell me. He'd say that hell is one of the greatest signs of God's love for us. He loves you and me so much that He will allow us to reject him for all eternity. He'd ask students: "How many of you have ever fallen in love with someone?" A number of kids would put up their hands. "And how many of you have ever fallen in love with someone who couldn't care less if you disappeared off the face of the earth, someone who totally rejected your love?" Some had experienced that. And he'd ask us: "Would you be happy with someone who was forced to love you?" And the answer was, of course, always 'no'. That's not a meaningful relationship. That's not genuine love. Love isn't love unless it is freely given. And if you truly love the person that you've fallen in love with, you will allow that person to reject your love; you would not force that person to love you.

Of course, God is Love. He is pure, absolute, love without limits. And He brought us into being precisely because He loves us, for love is effusive; it pours itself out, it extends beyond the self. More than that, He joined a human nature, entered into human suffering in order that we might not suffer alone and that our suffering might share in his redeeming influence and become a means to an eternal life of unimaginable joy in the Beatific Vision. And all He asks is that we receive the love that He has for us. All He asks is that we allow Him to love us, and then to love Him back. And He loves us so much that He will allow us to say 'no'.

And some people choose to say no. Some people freely choose to make themselves their own god, and those who do are not satisfied with being their own god; they want to be your god as well, and they won't rest until that happens.

There are certain characteristics that belong to those who love evil. The one predominant characteristic is that they are always well disguised and live behind a facade of goodness. They usually have most people in their immediate environment fooled. But the most important characteristic, which is well hidden, is that they have made themselves the absolute center of their own lives, and everybody else has been reduced to nothing more than a means to their own personal ends. Those who love evil are absolute egoists. The egoist loves himself as the absolute center, and everyone else is loved only insofar as they are of some use, that is, everyone else is on the periphery; they have nothing more than economic value.

There is a tremendous variety of people in this world, a tremendous variety of good people, and a tremendous variety of evil, that is, people who have made themselves the center of the universe. And there is tremendous evil in this world, but it is very difficult to uncover. The most insidious are in high places, the world of finance, and they live behind a facade of respectability, a facade of goodness. My awakening to evil was a very frightening and harrowing experience, and in the end, I came to realize how naive I had been about the nature of evil. I won't get into the details of that experience, but it lasted for a period of about six months; I discovered that someone in my life was a pathological narcissist who was not anything like many of us thought he was. But I also came to see the hand of divine providence in ways that I'd never before experienced.

Evil is fundamentally narcissistic. We have a tendency to project our own characteristics onto others, so if you are a deeply good human being, you tend to think everyone is, more or less. But there is real evil in the world, and it begins on the level of the human person; it begins with the free decisions of individual human persons to make themselves their own god, the measure of what is good and true, and not just for themselves—they are your god as well, and so they seek to dominate. Their egoism is such that they believe it is their mission in life to engineer society and the larger world according to their superior understanding of how the world should be and how history should unfold.

Evil is of its very nature deficient. It is a lack of something that should be there, as St. Augustine said. Evil is ugly, because it is a deficiency, an incompleteness, a lack. And so, the narcissist is spiritually unsightly to himself, and he knows that if others were to see him as he really is, they would be horrified, and they'd reject him. To make himself tolerable to himself—and so that he may feed off of the love and adulation of others—, he creates a facade, an image. And it is this image, this façade, that the narcissist loves. He does not love himself; he despises himself, hates what he has become, because evil is ugly and depraved. Rather, the narcissist loves the image he has created as a facade for others, an image that will procure a steady stream of fuel, the adulation of others, or, barring that, fear. This is the bread on which they live: the praise and adulation of others. The narcissist will not praise God, because in his mind, there is only one person who is deserving of praise, and that is himself. God is his competitor for attention, and every instant of his life will be aimed ultimately at procuring for himself what belongs to God.

And narcissists deliberately surround themselves with certain kinds of people, in particular, the excessively empathetic, those unwilling to judge; in short, those who are not shrewd. Narcissists need to be surrounded by people who will project their own goodness onto him. With such people, they are safe; the facade is safe. But they know who they are; they know they are sharks among porpoises, disguised wolves among sheep, cold creatures very different from the warm blooded. And because most people are overly credulous and lack shrewdness, the narcissist confidently schemes, plots, and like the brilliant chess player he plans a large number of moves ahead. He plots for power, for position, and God help the person who somehow manages to see through the facade. God help them because the narcissist has no conscience—it has been put in the freezer, so to speak.

Some of the best forensic psychologists and experts on psychopathology point out that it is very difficult to see through the facade of a genuine psychopath. And if you do, the tendency is to remain silent, because you see that he's got everyone fooled, and you'd come across as a nut if you were to explain what you know to others who are under his spell. Others feel indebted to him, they are enamored by his extraordinary personality, he's done so much good for others, hired them when no one else would, was good to them in a myriad of small ways. But his loyalty is paper thin. Others, however, cannot see that, because they project their own goodness onto him.

These narcissists have great influence over the naive and excessively empathetic. The empathetic don't want to disappoint, they don't want to betray, and they just do not behold the possibility that this person who has been so good to them has absolutely no love for them whatsoever. And so those who eventually see through the facade usually have to keep it to themselves, because few would believe them if they were to even suggest that this great man is not who everyone thinks he is; they would appear to so many others to be losing their minds.

But evil has no power, only the power that you and I lend it. And the source of that power lending is the disordered love we have for ourselves. If we love ourselves too much, in other words, if we love our job too much, so much so that we readily fall in line with groupthink, then we empower evil. If we are willing to compromise our conscience for the sake of our jobs, or for the sake of position, or for the sake of social acceptance, we empower the evil in this world. But evil would have no power without our cooperation. And sometimes we might choose to cooperate because we love our lives more than we love Truth and the Good. And then, at that point, we are capable of tremendous self-deception. We can erect very low confidence thresholds; for example, low acceptance thresholds for things we want to be true. This means that with just a bit of evidence, we accept this or that as true and good, because if we agree, it means a job or a promotion, or peer acceptance, and we correspondingly have high rejection thresholds for the same things, which means we demand mounds of evidence before we are willing to open up our eyes and see what's really there.

This is one thing that has really stood out for me after studying the clerical sex abuse scandals, in particular the abuse that took place in the 60s and 70s. A good number of narcissistic sociopaths were able to make it into the seminary and fool a good number of their fellow clergy, but what is particularly striking about this period is the support many of these abusers received from the wider community, its refusal to look at the evil among them. I'm referring to police officers, newspaper editors, judges, even federal judges, psychologists, doctors, and many parents who refused to believe the parents of abused children, in some cases even parents of the victims themselves, refusing to believe their sons and daughters. I was reminded of Dostoevsky's line in the Brothers Karamazov:

> There is only one way to salvation, and that is to make yourself responsible for all men's sins. As soon as you make yourself responsible in all sincerity for everything and for everyone, you will see at once that this is really so, and that you are in fact to blame for everyone and for all things.

I didn't always like that line; I was skeptical of it. I've had an oscillating relationship with it over the years: some days I'd see it and say, yes, that's true; other days, no, that's just not the case. But from one angle, we as a society really do create a social ethos, and in this social ethos is a moral anchor, and like any anchor, we do not veer too far away from it—only the brave are willing to veer far from it. We don't want to stand out. We let the wider social community define what is morally responsible, and here we fall into group think. Today we see this in the area of foreign policy and war, which is rarely talked about in mainstream media; I'm speaking of Afghanistan, Iraq, Libya, Syria, Yemen, and now there's a move on Venezuela and possibly Iran, but no one is allowed to talk about it, not even on Fox News. Prophets are lone voices; few pay attention to them because they do not have a wide social backing. There were some priests in the 60s and 70s who were whistleblowers and made known the abuse they were witnessing, but they suffered for it. The issues are different now, but the tendency to go along to get along, to be a team player for the sake of one's livelihood, has not really changed all that much.

But Jesus defeated the evil one again through the power of the word of God: *You shall worship the Lord, your God, and him alone shall you serve."* God alone is Truth Itself, Goodness Itself, and Beauty Itself.

We have the power, the ability, to rise above both the inclination to find our rest in the pleasures and goods of this world, and the disordered inclination to compromise our conscience for the sake of our own security, all because Christ defeated these two temptations in the wilderness. His victory is shared with us; the power of his will is shared with us.

That is what is so interesting about the Incarnation. By joining a human nature to himself, God the Son makes it possible for human beings to achieve his/her salvation; for a history is initiated in the Person of Christ, a history of the New Israel. The Incarnation creates a field of influence, so to speak, making it possible for other human persons to choose in

accordance with the will of God; the Incarnation makes
it possible to live within the mind and heart of Christ,
and the free choices of these very people in turn create
a field of influence that even has non local effects,
influencing others who may not even be within our
own vicinity. Just by growing in holiness, even in a
hidden way, we move this world forward. What
happens is that we enlarge that field of influence, an
invisible field, like a magnetic field, or better yet, the
quantum field. Just by living our life in the Person of
Christ, we influence the world in ways we cannot begin
to imagine—and it's an invisible influence. Because
Christ chose to put God before the bread and the glory
of this world, it is now possible for us to do just that.
We share in his power over evil. This is good news,
because the more we learn about the evil in this world,
the complicated network of financial schemes and
structures of power and control, it is easy to despair.
Most people don't have time to learn about such things,
and it can be frightening to do so, which is why so
many would simply rather not look into such things.
But the good news is that Christ began his defeat of evil
in the desert, at the very start of his ministry. Round

three is next, of course, the temptation to test God. All these are foreshadowings of his definitive defeat of evil on Good Friday, and our life in Christ is a participation in that victory, and that participation moves his victory through history, with an ever-widening influence, to its definitive conclusion. I believe one of the greatest joys in store for us in heaven will be to see just how wide and extensive our influence was.

Trusting in Providence

> *Then he led him to Jerusalem, made him stand on the parapet of the temple, and said to him, "If you are the Son of God, throw yourself down from here, for it is written: He will command his angels concerning you, to guard you, and: With their hands they will support you, lest you dash your foot against a stone."*
>
> *Jesus said to him in reply, "It also says, You shall not put the Lord, your God, to the test." When the devil had finished every temptation, he departed from him for a time.*

The devil now moves to attack the word of God that Jesus uses to defeat him. Throw yourself down, for Scripture says His angels will support you. As if to say: Let's test the veracity of the Scriptures. Here the devil attempts to draw Jesus into the arrogance of testing God, subjecting God to the measuring of human reason; let us subject God to experiment, treat Him as though He were a hypothesis that requires testing. Test God rather than trust God.

The devil implies that God is a liar, as he did in the Garden: "Did God really say that you are not to eat of the trees in the garden? The woman answered: "We may eat of the fruit of the trees in the garden, just not the fruit of the tree in the middle of the garden. God said, 'You shall not eat of it or even touch it; if you do, you will die. But the serpent replied: 'No, you will not die'. The devil implies that God deceives, that He cannot be trusted.

The devil is the father of lies, and he assures us that God lies, which means it is a lie that God lies, which in turn means God does not lie. And one who does not lie is trustworthy, and God is pre-eminently trustworthy. The devil constantly works to sow doubt in God's trustworthiness.

But the only way to know that God does not lie is to trust first. This reminds me of St. Augustine, who said: "Believe in order to understand". Do not try to understand in order to believe. Many will refuse to believe until they understand, until they are assured of the truth of the faith. But St. Augustine points out that the condition for understanding the truths of the faith is believing, that is, trusting. Faith begets knowledge and understanding, which are Gifts of the Holy Spirit.

And this is true when it comes to natural faith as well. For example, you will never understand love, that is, the love another has for you, unless you take a risk and trust that person when he or she says: 'I love you'.

You will never know that love without an act of faith.
So too, if an individual person does not trust that God
is in control, that He supports her, carries her, watches
over her, protects her, she will never know it from
within. The gift of knowledge, one of the gifts of the
Holy Spirit, is the ability to see the hand of providence
in our day to day existence; we actually experience
God's providential hand, governing events, especially
our own life. If we do not trust, then we move to take
control of things ourselves; we attempt to micromanage
our life, and the lives of others in our immediate
environment. We scheme to make things work our way.
And that's when things go wrong, and we never really
come to understand from within that God can be
trusted.

Just recently I had an experience that reminded me
of this very point. We have a chapel in our school, a
beautiful chapel, and some students are regulars in that
chapel—some teachers as well. But for the past three
years or so, an East Indian girl would come in every
morning and find a spot in the corner and devoutly
pray by herself. I didn't know who she was. This year I
just happened to walk down the hall and noticed her

walking beside me, so I turned and said: "Hello, how are you?" Of course, we knew each other only as chapel buddies. I asked her: "What grade are you in?" She said, "grade 12". I asked her if she was taking philosophy, and she said no, she's taking the grade 12 religion. So, I said to her, "You should take philosophy; you'd enjoy it". And then I left to do whatever it was I was going to do. A couple of days later, she arrives at my classroom and asks whether I am teaching philosophy in period 1. I said I was; She said, "I'm going to go to the guidance department and see if I can get into this course". "Wonderful", I said.

A few days later I saw her in the halls and asked her whether she got in, but she said she did not, because the class was full. I was somewhat disappointed, and later I was tempted to go down to guidance and tell the department head to just put her in my class and not to worry about the numbers. Then I thought: if she's not on my list, God has other plans, so best to accept the order of providence as it is. The next day I noticed that some students had their schedules changed and were forced to drop the course, which is quite normal at the start of a semester. So, I thought:

why don't I go down and tell our head of guidance: "Remember the East Indian girl who tried to get into my class a few days ago, can you change her schedule again and add her to my class list, if there is an opening?" But then I thought I'd better not; providence did not arrange to have her in my class, so I'd better not try to manipulate things to work out a certain way. The next day, however, she arrives in my class and shows me her new schedule—she was added to the list. I didn't have to micromanage anything.

When we let God act, He acts in the best interests of everyone. If we try to take control, manipulate, lie, scheme, we push God to the side as if to say: "I don't trust you". And we do things our way, and the result is the world as it is at this point.

The problem with control is that the world is far too complex for us to manipulate. The economy, which is only one small aspect of this world, is a perfect example. Good economists will tell you that an economy is not like an automobile engine that can be diagnosed and fixed; it is far too complicated. There are no simple solutions to economic problems, only trade-offs, and no single human being or bureaucracy has the intellectual capacity to understand all that is necessary to understand in order to manage an economy. That is why central-planners always fall short and, in the end, do more damage than good. Human beings are far too limited intellectually, and the information required to diagnose and repair an economy exceeds human intellectual capacity. And that's why we have guardian angels—because we are so slow.

If we study the history of science, we see that the progress of science is very slow, and this is all because human intelligence is profoundly limited. We are very slow to discover not because truth is so hard to grasp— truth is really quite simple. Rather, it takes centuries to *discover* these truths because human beings are intellectually sluggish; it is matter and sense perception that profoundly limit human intelligence. This is what I try to get across to my students, in particular those who are relatively bright; they learn, in the course of a semester, what it took the most brilliant minds centuries to discover. They learn calculus in a semester, conditional probabilities, physics, biology, chemistry, all in the course of a semester or two, but achieving that level of discovery took centuries for the most brilliant minds to get there. Why? Because we are so slow. It does not take centuries to learn that material, only to discover it.

I'm always surprised at this when I teach something like ethics or the basics of logic, or some other branch of philosophy. For me, what I am teaching them is very simple material; it's not really hard at all. And yet the same kids who have taken calculus, or physics, or chemistry, or complicated mathematics, are having a hard time wrapping their heads around what I'm teaching them. And I too remember struggling to learn certain concepts that I now know are really very simple.

Although man is the highest creature on the hierarchy of being in the physical universe—we are superior to animals, who are in turn superior to plants, which are in turn superior to non-living matter—, we are the lowest of God's intellectual creatures. Angels are far superior to man. And there is a hierarchy of angels. At the very top are the Seraphim, and below them are the Cherubim angels, and then the Thrones. The next hierarchy are made up of the Dominations, the Celestial Virtues, and the Powers, and finally, on the lowest hierarchy, there are the principalities, the archangels, and the angels. The name Seraphim means "carriers of fire". The Cherubim, who are below the Seraphim, are the most intelligent of God's intellectual creatures, for the name means "fullness of knowledge". Why are the Seraphim higher than the Cherubim? The best answer I have found is that in Scripture, fire is a symbol of the divine love—God is a consuming fire, according to the letter to the Hebrews. If we get too close to a fire, we will catch on fire. The Seraphim are so close to God that they have caught on fire, so to speak; they burn with the fire of the divine love. The Seraphim are highest because love of God is greater than knowledge. It is said that Lucifer was a Cherubim angel; for he was the "most cunning animal that the Lord God had made" (Gn 3, 1). Cunning is an intellectual quality; it points to one who is conniving, and the devil is extraordinarily clever in a devious way. The principalities are the guardians of nations, the archangels are the guardians of important personages, leaders of state, bishops, popes, etc., and the angels, the lowest choir on the hierarchy, are guardians of ordinary persons. Our guardian angel is far superior intellectually than the most brilliant human being.

Man, however, is not an angel, but he is an intellectual creature, and we are on the lowest rung of the intellectual ladder. We are like brute animals in that we have sensation and sense appetite, and we are like the angels insofar as we have a mind that possesses ideas. But our knowledge begins with sense perception, and so it is slow in developing, unlike that of an angel.

The glory of man is not intelligence; angels do not envy our intelligence. Intelligence is the glory of the angels. We can't outdo them in intelligence; in other words, we won't be able to teach our own guardian angel anything. Rather, man's glory is humility. And that's precisely what angels envy in us, our potentiality for humility. The word 'human' comes from the Latin *humus*, which means dirt, earth, soil. Man is from the earth; he is limited by matter. The word humor also comes from the same root (*humus*). A humble man is able to laugh at himself, he sees the humor in being human, subject to error. A humble man is "down to earth" (*humus*), has his feet on the ground, he does not walk high and mighty, he does not see himself as superior, but is aware of his limitations and vulnerability to destruction. We can outdo the angels in humility; Mary did, which is why she is Queen of Angels. She is inferior to the angels in her nature, but she is superior to angels in the order of divine grace. She is full of grace. She says in the Magnificat: "The Lord has looked upon the *nothingness* of his servant" (Lk 1, 48). She sees her nothingness. Not an ounce of pride, not even the slightest sense of superiority, and she is the mother of God and queen of angels.

Intelligence is not our glory. Knowledge is very hard to achieve, and most of what is in our heads is not knowledge at all, but belief, the result of natural faith, in the sense of believing what someone tells you because you have evidence of his credibility and trustworthiness. For example, the doctor writes a prescription for us, tells us to take this until the bottle is empty. We trust her; we don't "know" that she has our best interest in mind, but we believe she does. We trust the pharmacist, that he hasn't made a mistake and that this medication is not going to kill us. I don't know what these pills are, I haven't studied biochemistry and pharmacology. I trust, I believe, I put my faith in him. And not even the pharmacist who has studied pharmacology and biochemistry, etc., really knows that everything he prescribes is good for the patient; he trusts the research. We trust our mechanic when he assures us that he fixed our brakes and added the right amount of brake fluid. I don't demand that he hoist the car up, take off the wheels and show me. I get in and drive. I'll know if my trust was well placed when I get to a red light or a stop sign. If my brakes don't work, I'll know then that he's not trustworthy. My students trust me whenever I teach them anything about the history of philosophy or religion or the fundamentals of ethics. I could be lying to them, making it all up; they don't know, they trust. The world of science also relies heavily upon faith; no scientist can repeat every experiment, or every formal study done in the past, not even the most recent studies. Scientists trust that data has not been falsified. But that trust has been betrayed in the past.

The fact is we simply can't function without faith; we are too limited. We have to rely on others, we have no choice but to trust them, and at times that trust is betrayed. And what would life look like without it? Children believe their parents when they are told that brushing their teeth is good for them, but imagine a child who refuses to trust his parents and demands proof before doing anything: "I don't trust you that this food is edible", or "…that this toothpaste won't harm me". That would be strange, wouldn't it? A marriage relationship is based on faith. You just don't know whether or not this person really loves you or whether he's lying and is just using you. He says he loves you, and you trust him, you put your faith in him; and that's the beauty of genuine love—it is based on natural faith, but faith is risky. What kind of relationship is based on complete and total security? Certainly not love.

Although faith is an act of the intellect, behind it is a decision, an act of the will, an act of love. And although 95% of the things we do is based on natural faith, and although we are too ready to put our faith in all sorts of people, some of whom we should not trust, for some reason, many find it very difficult to trust God.

In this third temptation in the desert, Jesus is tempted to test God. He defeats the devil without any effort, but that specific temptation assails every human being, especially those who are relatively intelligent. We are tempted, behind a facade of intellectual brilliance and sophistication, to treat God as though He were a hypothesis that needs to measure up to our high standards of acceptance. We forget how much of our day to day life is based on faith, on natural faith, and why it is based on faith—the reason being that are so limited and deficient intellectually.

To put our faith in God is very fitting, perfectly congruent with human nature and the nature of human knowing. If coming to understand the nature of things in this world is so difficult because the world is so complex and varied and we are so slow, how much more difficult is it to come to understand something of God, who is Truth Itself, Goodness Itself, Beauty Itself, God whose essence is to exist necessarily and eternally. It is not up to us to test God, but to trust God. This can be very difficult to do in times of darkness, especially a darkness caused by a personal tragedy. Personal tragedies affect some people's faith more than others. For some, their faith is strengthened; for others, they may give up their faith in anger. I'm not here to judge such people, but I can put forth the following thought experiment: imagine a very wealthy person suddenly entering your life and telling you that $100,000 is going to be automatically deposited into your bank account every month for an as yet undetermined period of time. You don't know when, but one day the cash flow will stop. It may stop after a year, or it may continue for a decade or two. If it continues, you will have received a million dollars within the year. He doesn't tell you why. In fact, there is no reason. He just decides to do this.

Why do I bring this up? We know from Exodus that God is "He Who Is" (Yahweh). On the basis of this text, Aquinas argues that God *is* His own Act of Existing, whereas the rest of us in creation only *have* a received existence. I *am* human (that's my nature), but I *have* existence (existence is not my nature). God on the other hand *is* His Existence. He is pure being. And God is the First Existential Cause of everything that has existence, whether it be a thought, a meson, a photon of light, the Higgs field, a human person, or an angel. Now over the years I've met some young people who have lost loved ones very close to them. Some of these people responded to their loss by drawing closer to God, while others became angry with God and consequently cut themselves off from the sacraments. Again, I have no intention of judging the latter. But I do offer a thought. A person cannot be in debt if the creditor does not exist. In other words, God cannot incur debt. Existence is sheer gift. It is not possible to earn the right to exist; for if one does not exist, one cannot earn anything. Everything we have from God is pure gift, given *gratis*, that is, without our having earned any of it, not even the slightest moment of time. If God chooses to give my daughter only 5 years, I cannot justifiably claim that God owes her more, any more than I can demand that the $100,000 I have been receiving monthly be continued for another ten years or so, or any more than I can demand 30 million instead of 15 million. That money was given *gratis*. It was all bonus. It belongs to someone who has chosen to share it with me, without my having any right to it. I do not have a claim on the source. Similarly, my life does not belong to me, but to God. Should I or my daughter or my brother be called home after 25 years, or 15 years, or even 5 years, no one can accuse God of depriving me, or her, or him, of what is rightfully mine, hers, or his. Everything was bonus from the start.

My daughter has been entrusted to me, not for my sake, but for hers; for she is not my right, but a trust. A human being cannot be made an object of a right; a child is a gift, the supreme gift of matrimony. To make a child the object of a right is to violate the requirement that other human persons be treated in a way that respects their status as equal in dignity to myself. And so, it is on the basis of this trust that I am bound by obligation; but not God. My life has been entrusted to me; and so my own body is not, properly speaking, my own. It is on the basis of this trust that I am bound by duty to protect my life, to revere it and preserve it. But God is not bound by duty; for everything I have from Him in life is bonus, that is, pure gift.

I contend that the reason so many people are not nearly as happy as they could be is that they go through life without the explicit awareness that everything in their lives is pure gift. There is something wrong with the way some people see and interpret the world around them. Our very life in the flesh is gift; our friends are gift, education is gift, health and our own intelligence is gift, and parents are gift, and the most developmentally disabled child is gift, sent to us from

God as an invitation to love that child for his or her own sake, and in doing so, to be more fully conformed to God, who is Love.

Like the child, people have to have this pointed out to them, but pointing it out is never enough. It must become a personal insight. When we really see that all is gift, we will turn to God with a desire to "thank" Him, and our thanks will contain a genuine experience of the joy of God, who is His own Joy. A longing to thank Him every day will arise within us, and every day we will taste a small portion of the joy of heaven.

This return to God is the essence of religion. The religious spirit is a spirit of thanks. And what is particularly remarkable about this is that as we turn to God, we discover that He turns towards us, drawing closer to us, thus giving us more of Himself: "If you turn to him with all your heart and with all your soul, to do what is true before him, then he will turn to you and will no longer hide his face from you" (Tb 13, 6). In this way our debt continually increases, and so too our desire to thank Him and enter more fully into His Joy. For He gives us His body, blood, soul and divinity in the Eucharist at every Mass. The very word "Eucharist" means thanksgiving. It is Christ in the act of perfect worship of His Father; it is the sacrifice of the cross, the most perfect religious act, the reconciliation of the human race to God. It is this perfect act of religion that brings eternal life to those who enter into it. The Eucharist is our entry into the heart of God.

It is impossible to ever satisfy the debt we owe to God, but as we try, He goes further by refusing to allow us to lessen the balance by replying to all our attempts with greater blessings. When a person first chooses to turn to God in an act of religion, he has no idea of the blessings that he opens up for himself and for all those who are and will be a part of his life.

And this brings us to the Beatitudes, each one of which begins with *makarios*, translated as blessed, or happy. It is a unique kind of happiness. This is a happiness that is complete and sufficient unto itself. It is the first taste of eternal life. Human happiness is precarious, it is risky, dependent upon so many factors of which we have no control. But *makarios* is entirely different; it is other worldly. It is supernatural. It is the joy of being supported by God; it is a sharing in His happiness. It is a kind of happiness that no external circumstance can diminish, unlike human happiness or contentment—the stock market can crash, banks can fail, we can lose our job, come down with cancer, etc. Memories fade, people forget us, especially after we are gone. What good are all our awards and accolades then? Any happiness that is dependent upon circumstances beyond our control is not the happiness we were made for. Rather, we were created for *makarios*, blessedness. It is not happiness, much less is it pleasure. It is a taste of eternal life, the joy of heaven, here and now, and it is not diminished by physical pain, nor is it diminished by unfortunate circumstances. It is the happiness that results from taking on the mind of Christ. And the basic contours of that mind are outlined in the Beatitudes in the fifth chapter of the gospel of Matthew.

> *Blessed are the poor in spirit; the kingdom of heaven is theirs.*

This is the first condition for *makarios*, that blessedness that cannot really be described. To be poor in spirit is to be aware of one's radical need for God. A person who is poor in wealth knows it; he knows his lack, he tastes it every day. The one who is poor in spirit knows his spiritual lack, his utter need for God.

One of my greatest blessings as a deacon is being able to minister to those who suffer from mental illness. This ministry is not about counselling or offering any kind of therapy. Rather, it is about visitation—in fact, I was ordained on the feast of the Visitation, which celebrates Mary's visit to her cousin Elizabeth, during which John the Baptist leapt for joy in Elizabeth's womb. The word 'visit' comes from the Latin *visitare*, which means to go to see, from *visere*, which means to behold. To visit a person is to notice them, to look at them a certain way. My ministry is simply to look at them, to behold them. Early on in my teaching career I had a recurring dream: I kept dreaming of a teacher I had in the seventh grade; a French teacher. And all he was doing in the dream was looking at me, as he did back then. He had a nice smile, but as I was thinking about it back then, I realized that it was a look that saw something in me, and it taught me to see, preconsciously, that same something in me as well. I believe that is why I would always wake up in a spirit of joy. Very early on as a teacher, I realized that more fundamental than the teaching of the curriculum was the way I beheld my students. How do I look at them? Do I behold their dignity? Do I see them as God sees them? If I do, they will know it; they will come to know who they are through that gaze. It's all about how you look at them. That's my ministry to those who suffer from mental illness.

I bring them up because those in my life who have been the most spiritually poor have been those who suffer from mental illness. And it is no coincidence that they have a depth that is lacking to a great many who do not suffer from mental illness. It's a very painful gift, a very painful vocation, but I do believe with Carrol Houselander that mental illness really is a vocation. Allow me to read from an article she wrote entitled: *The Care of the Mentally Ill:*

> ...For he [the mental sufferer], by his unique suffering, is taking part in the world's redemption.
> This must never be forgotten. The mental sufferer must never be regarded as one whose life is without purpose or meaning, as a burden to his family, or as one who gives nothing to those who care for him, because he is in fact giving the

redeeming suffering of Christ, on which the
salvation of the world and each one of us
depends.[1]

The first condition for possessing the kingdom of
heaven is poverty of spirit, the recognition and
acceptance of one's own utter need for God. When life
is too good, when things are going so well and we feel
on top of the world, we tend to lose a sense of our
vulnerability to destruction and the shortness and
brevity of human life. We lose a sense of our own
absence of control. When things do not go our way and
life becomes difficult, the sense of our absence of
control is acute. And that is the problem with being
young; young people are strong, their bodies heal
quickly, they have lots of energy and they have
powerful imaginations, but they have very little
experience in being wrong—for they have very little
experience. I always tell my students that I have far
more experience in being wrong than they have; I've
had 57 years of experience in being wrong, mistaken,
having rushed to judgment, believing the world was a

---

[1] *The Mother of Christ*, New York: Sheed and Ward, 1978. p. 97.

certain way, only to discover ten years later that it isn't, believing everyone is good willed only to discover twenty years later that it is not the case at all, believing that this person is completely wrong about this or that issue, only to discover thirty years later that it is I who was wrong all along, not them, etc. They only have 17 or 18 years of experience, and they are not very aware of just how much they've been wrong in that short time. When we are young, we tend to believe our grasp of reality is far more comprehensive than it really is, and it takes experience to eventually realize that we know virtually nothing and that what we know is infinitely tiny compared to how much more there is to know and how much more there is to reality that is knowable but hidden from us. It was physicist Richard Feynman who regarded science as an ever-expanding frontier of ignorance: the more we discover, the more we come to realize how much more there is to know.

And so, it is indeed the case that those circumstances in our lives that bring home the fundamental truth about man, namely that we are poor in spirit, utterly in need to God's constant providence, are real gifts. Sickness can be a genuine gift that makes a higher joy possible in our lives, and that higher joy is *makarios*. Even the word ecstasy is revealing. It comes from the Greek *ekstasis*, which means 'beside oneself', or 'outside oneself', which also includes insanity, as in 'he's out of his mind'. A person can be so ecstatic that he's beside himself. What the word really points to is an 'exit of self'. One leaves oneself. Genuine love is ecstatic: it involves an exit of self, a movement towards the other not for the sake of oneself, but for the other's sake. Pleasure is not really ecstatic, because pleasure is *in the self,* and so a life of pleasures is not necessarily a joyful life. The pleasure ends when the source of that pleasure ceases to act upon us, or shortly thereafter. But joy endures, and joy is only discovered through an exit of self, through a decision to forget the self in order to consider the other for that person's sake. It does not get old. Excitement gets old, but not joy.

But the kind of life put forth by contemporary popular culture today is not a life that will procure joy. Rather, today life is for the most part about excitement and the pleasure of novelties. But novelties in time cease to be novelties, and so one has to search for new and exciting experiences. And that kind of existence is incompatible with commitment. Commitment is long range. It is in for the long haul. Things might be exciting at first, because they are new, but that soon wears off; genuine love, on the other hand, commits to the other for the other's sake, and so it is not about excitement. It can handle boredom; it is prepared for boredom. A life of committed love is very much like working on a painting. It might be exciting at first, but that wears off and it soon becomes tedious, slow moving, and it demands great patience. What sustains one is the realization that one is producing a work of beauty. An individual life is supposed to be a work of beauty in which there is a finished product that one can present to God, a meaningful work that can last an eternity. But a life that is nothing more than a stream of pleasures and excitements is like a firework display; it's enjoyable while it lasts, but there is no enduring meaning. When I lived in Montreal, they used to have the world fireworks competition. We'd walk to the harbourfront and sit down to watch the display of the country whose night it was: Mexico, Canada, France, Japan, the United States, etc. The U.S of course was always the loudest, sounding as if bombs are being dropped on us, as if we're in the middle of a war; Japan was always elegant, Canada was very reserved, etc. Those nights were fun, but we felt the emptiness at the end; there's nothing really memorable, unlike beholding a masterpiece or listening to a great symphony or reading a great novel. A life that is nothing more than a stream of excitements and pleasures is really like that in the end. There is nothing to present to God after it is all over; it was a life lived entirely for the self. It is a tragic life. But a life of suffering that shares directly in the mystery of redemption, which is essentially what the life of a person with mental illness is—in particular a person who has accepted that suffering—, is a profoundly meaningful life whose meaning will only be fully revealed at judgment, and that will be a moment of indescribable joy.

Mental sufferers have a special vocation that is a participation in the mystery of Holy Thursday night. Christ entered the Garden of Gethsemane and suffered mental anguish. He took Peter, James, and John with him and told them to stay awake with him one hour. They could not do it. But those who suffer with clinical depression, anxiety, paranoia or any other mental illness, do keep Christ company in his suffering. He does not suffer alone; you suffer with him, and he accompanies you in the depths of your suffering. When we are suffering, it is always comforting to know there is someone nearby who accompanies us. This is the gift that mental sufferers bring to Christ throughout their lives, and the knowledge of that will be a source of joy and meaning.

But you may not be suffering from a mental illness. Nevertheless, if you've loved, if you've lived a life of committed love, you've suffered. If you've raised children, and if you've loved those children, you've done incalculable good, but at the same time it was a difficult life. And as Christ offers his crucified life to the Father, we too offer our life of love and suffering to the Father for Him to do with as He pleases. And He is pleased with His Son, which is why He accepted His offering and raised Him up. And He too will be pleased with your offering because it was a life lived in the Person of Christ. He sees His Son in your life, and so He is pleased with it; and He will respond the same way by raising you up.

It's this idea that the Father sees His Son in our suffering that I find intriguing. I had an experience that I think might illustrate this. A few years ago my daughter, wife and I went to Italy with friends of ours who are Italian—and who drive like Italians. They took us north, and south, all throughout, and my daughter loved it. She was, however, focused primarily on shopping. I hated going in to shops to look for purses or dresses, I just wanted to explore the narrow streets and the Churches around almost every corner, so for me it was a very unpleasant trip: it was hot, and I was always watching out for pickpockets, there was not enough time to visit the places I wanted to visit, and I actually did lose 100 euros. I believe I was robbed by the hotel in which I was staying—I can't prove that, but there's no other explanation. They probably saw how much I ate at the continental breakfast and decided I needed to pay extra. Other than the pastries, I found it to be a very unpleasant trip.

The following year, however, I got to go again, this time without my wife and daughter, just a priest friend of mine and a good friend who is also a teacher and whose parents own an apartment in Rome; so, we spent two weeks there. What I found fascinating upon reflection was that I spent so much time visiting the fashion district, Via Del Corso, the clothing stores, looking for dresses and purses, etc. I was doing a lot of shopping for my daughter, to bring things back for her, and I was enjoying it. I wanted to visit the places that she loved. I started to love these places, because there was something of her that was left behind. I couldn't care less about the Trevi Fountain or the Spanish Steps, but because she loved those places, the next year I made sure to visit them, but only because I was looking to recapture her presence. These places were dear to her, so they became dear to me.

God the Son joined a human nature. The lost human race was dear to him as a lost sheep is dear to the shepherd, and he went looking for us. He walked our streets, he lived our life, he entered into human suffering. God the Father sees His Son in the human nature he joined and in the human life he embraced. He looks at us because He wishes to behold the image of His Son, the presence of His Son that is there in the persons of those who are poor in spirit, in the persons of those who love the poor and who in turn see Christ in the poor of this world.

The Victory is Ours

> *Thus says the Lord: Just as from the heavens the rain and snow come down and do not return there till they have watered the earth, making it fertile and fruitful, giving seed to the one who sows and bread to the one who eats, so shall my word be that goes forth from my mouth; it shall not return to me void, but shall do my will, achieving the end for which I sent it.* (Is 55, 10-11)

This is a very hopeful reading. What it says essentially is that evil will not have the final word over our lives. God's Word went forth from his mouth, and that Word is the Second Person of the Trinity, the *Logos* who was made flesh and dwelt among us and whose blood, poured out on the earth, was seed that penetrated into the soil of the ground; from that ground will spring life, and that life will proliferate throughout history and will accomplish what Christ set out to accomplish. And what he set out to accomplish is right there in today's Responsorial Psalm: "From all their distress God rescues the just." And the psalm says: "Glorify the Lord with me, let us together extol his name".

There are two sides to Christ's coming: He came to glorify God and to extol his name, and he came to save us, to rescue us, to give us a share in the supernatural life of grace. He came so that we might be able to participate in the inner life of the Trinity, rather than live outside that life in darkness, leading lives that are, in the end, futile and ultimately pointless.

The cross is the glorification of the Father, and it is the sign of his power over evil. On one side, the cross reveals the glory of the divine love, the love that Christ has for the Father and for us. And it reveals the power of God. God is so powerful that He can defeat the one enemy that we cannot defeat, namely death, and he defeated this enemy by dying, by allowing death to have victory over him. By allowing death to swallow him, he defeats death. He injects death with his own divine life such that suffering and death can now impart his life. The Word is joined to "human" suffering and dying and thus can be discovered there. Death's victory is death's defeat. And Christ shares his victory with us. It is our victory now.

Man is a work of God. We exist in the image and likeness of God. To stray from the law of God, to sin, is to distort that image, to make ourselves ugly and miserable. To stray from the law of God reflects badly on the divine image, and so Christ came to restore that reflection, to beauty us, to take away our misery. The cross is the paradoxical image of the beauty of God, the beauty of the divine love, and we take on that beauty the more we share in his cross.

At the beginning of every semester, I will often ask students if they know the secret to looking beautiful, and of course they have no clue. So I tell them a story that happened to me back when I first began to teach at Father Michael McGivney. I was in my early 40s, 41 or 42, I remember that my memory was starting to go at that time—I couldn't recall what I had for supper the previous nights, not to mention other things that were never a problem before. I'd share that with my students, remind them that every day that passes they are 24 hours closer to the grave—try to cheer them up. But one student decided to take advantage of my deteriorating memory. I had given out an assignment on *The Apology of Socrates*. They had to read it and answer questions, and the assignment was worth a lot. I collected them and marked them. One student did very well, but two students just didn't do the assignment, so I had to assign a mark of zero. I was disappointed, because it was going to affect their mid-term mark. The next day I handed back their work and then went on with the class. But the following day, a young girl, very pretty and who could easily do well in modelling, she said to me: "Sir, you handed me my assignment the other day, but you didn't put a mark on it."

"No mark? I must have forgotten to put a mark on this. I'll take it home, look on my computer and let you know what you got," I said.

When I got home, I discovered that she was one of the students who got a zero, because she didn't hand it in. I thought perhaps I read it but forgot to actually put the mark on it, so I began to read it and I noticed that it was very well written, very thorough, and there was only one other student who wrote that well. Of course, he sat right next to her.

Now I have a very good verbal memory; I know when I've read something before, so I was quite sure that she simply borrowed the essay of the person sitting next to her. So the following day I saw that boy who got a very good mark, he was walking down the hall towards me. I said to him:

"Stop. I have a question for you, and I want a simple yes or no answer, and no matter how you answer, you are not going to get in trouble. I promise. I am just going to send you on your way. No chance of getting in trouble. But I want the truth, just a yes or no".

He agreed, so I asked him: "Did you lend your paper to (name) for her to copy?"

"Yes", he said.

"Thank you very much. Go on your merry way and enjoy your lunch".

I then had the office page her to go to my room.

I was angry only because she took lying to a new level. Students lie all the time, i.e., my printer broke, my mother's car wouldn't start, etc., but they never get the teacher involved. She, however, said that I did something, when I did not: you handed back this paper to me but forgot to put a mark on it. That's what bothered me.

She arrived at the door. "You said that I gave this back to you when I was handing them back to the class", I said.

"Yes, you did Sir".

"Are you sure?"

"Yes, you did Sir".

"You know, my memory is getting bad, but it's not that bad, at least not yet. Are you sure I gave this back to you?"

"Yes, you did, Sir".

"You know, I have a very good verbal memory, and I was reading this, and it is very well done. But I am pretty sure I never read this before. I don't think I handed this back to you".

She continued with the denials, but I could sense that her resolve was weakening. She probably began to wonder whether I actually knew.

And then I looked up at her. What I saw astounded me. I didn't recognize her. That natural beauty of hers thinned out. Her eyes brows were crooked, her mouth was slightly different. I really didn't recognize her at first.

And then I thought that this is what Oscar Wilde was getting at in *The Picture of Dorian Gray*, that you wear your character on your face. The eyes are the windows of the soul, as they say. She was not that pretty young girl at that moment. Something was missing in her countenance. A fullness was missing. The secret to looking beautiful is character. In other words, the secret to looking beautiful is virtue.

Aristotle knew it more than 2000 years ago. In his great work *The Nicomachean Ethics*, he has a word, the *kalon*, which is very difficult to translate in English. The *kalon* has often been translated as the morally right, the morally good, the noble, but these do not capture the complete meaning of the Greek word. *Kalon* comes from *kaleo*, which means attractive; what is attractive draws a person; *kaleo* is a fundamental property of beautiful works of art. The *kalon* is best translated as "the morally beautiful". But that expression is odd in the English language. We think of moral goodness as fulfilling our duties, taking the most difficult and unpleasant course of action. In our minds, it has nothing to do with beauty. But not for Aristotle. Moral nobility means moral beauty. The virtuous course of action is the morally beautiful course of action.

According to Aristotle, the human person is a unity of spirit and matter. The soul is not inside the body, as it was for Plato and Socrates. Rather, the body is in the soul. Body and soul are two principles of a single substance. So, what happens on the level of the soul affects the body, especially the countenance (the face). Virtue beautifies and brings harmony to the 11 basic emotions of the human being, subjecting them to human reason, and harmony is one of the properties of beauty. The virtues beautify the soul, and since soul and body are intimately linked as two distinct principles of a single substance, a beautiful soul will influence a person's matter, especially the matter of the face.

And so, it is possible to fall in love with a great looking guy with a good six pack, nice hair, tall, athletic, etc., but after you get to know his character, which might be egotistical and self-centered, what happens is that he becomes less attractive to you. And conversely, take someone who is mediocre, not strikingly handsome or pretty, but has tremendous moral character, wouldn't sell her soul for anything. Such a person becomes increasingly attractive.

Virtue, moral goodness, holiness, is the secret to looking beautiful. That's why I love parent/teacher interviews. I get to meet parents, and some of the parents of our students have great faces. I don't mean a pretty face or a handsome face, but a good face. You can have a rather ugly face, one that no modelling agency would be interested in, but have a great face. And you can have a handsome face, or pretty face, but a bad face. Lots of models do in fact.

Divine grace beautifies the soul, endowing it with an "other-worldly" beauty. People of real holiness and integrity, no matter how old, always have great faces; radiant with moral beauty. Christ came to restore that supernatural beauty that was lost through sin and rebellion. Jesus said:

In my Father's house, there are many mansions.

Hearing this line (Jn 14, 1-12), I often think of the time I visited Trinity Retreat Center in Larchmont, New York, a retreat house that was, at the time, run by

Father Benedict Groeschel. Between talks we'd have time to go for walks around Larchmont, one of the richest neighborhoods in the United States. My spiritual director grew up in Brooklyn, and he too visited Trinity Retreat Center, and he recalls walking around the Yacht Club, enjoying the boats, the water, and the mansions. He asked his friend who was with him:

"If you had your choice, which mansion would you want?"

And he would reply: "Oh, if I had my choice, I'd want to live in that one over there".

My spiritual director then said: "Well if I had my choice, I'd want to live in that one over there", pointing to one in the opposite direction.

Just a few feet away from them, sitting on a park bench, was an older lady, and as he said those words, she perked up and said: "No, you would not want to live in that house over there. I live in that house over there, and that's why I'm sitting here".

"In my Father's house, there are many mansions" clearly does not mean literally mansion or house. St. John of the Cross, the great 16th century Spanish mystic, wrote in the first line of his famous poem: *The*

Why Are You Afraid?

Ascent of Mount Carmel:

> On a dark night, Kindled in love with yearnings –
> oh, happy chance! – I went forth without being
> observed, my house being now at rest.

The house he refers to is his entire soul, which includes the emotions, the intellect and the will. His "house being now at rest" means he has brought order to soul: the emotions are subject to reason and will, which in turn are subject to God. We build our house with every choice that we make, and we have to live in that house. When someone does something seriously wrong, like murder or fraud, and gets away with it, others will often say things like: "How can you stand to look at yourself in the mirror?" or "How can you live with yourself?" No matter how much money you have, if you can't live with yourself, if you don't like what you have become, then it makes no difference what kind of a house you live in or how large a piece of property you have, because the house that Jesus is talking about is the interior dwelling place of your own soul, and either God dwells there or he does not.

In the book of Revelations, we read:

You keep saying, "I am so rich and secure that I want for nothing." Little do you realize how wretched you are, how pitiable and poor, how blind and naked! Take my advice. Buy from me gold refined by fire if you would be truly rich. Buy white garments in which to be clothed, if the shame of your nakedness is to be covered. Buy ointment to smear on your eyes, if you would see once more. Whoever is dear to me I reprove and chastise. Be earnest about it, therefore. Repent! Here I stand, knocking at the door. If anyone hears me calling and opens the door, I will enter his house and have supper with him, and he with me. (Rev 3, 17-20)

If Christ is not there dining with us, then we are alone, no matter how many people we have surrounding us. The mansion he speaks about in this verse is the heart. The heart is the will, and the will establishes our moral identity, and moral identity is what we mean by character, the kind of person that you and I have made ourselves to be by the moral choices that we have made in life and continue to make every day. Every time we make a morally significant choice, in part we shape a moral identity. We are building our eternal mansion here and now through those very choices. If I choose to steal, I become a thief—that's who I am, even if no one knows about it; if I choose to lie, I become a liar, and if I choose to kill, I am a killer, etc. I am reminded of a film produced years ago by TV Ontario, a film on Euthanasia in Holland. In it, a doctor was interviewed who would euthanize patients if they requested it. He said he had to take off his white coat every time he would euthanize a patient, and he didn't know why. The reason, of course, is that at that moment, he's no longer a doctor; a doctor heals, cares for his patients, keeps them as comfortable as possible, he does not murder them. The word medical comes from the Latin *medicor*, which means 'to heal', to 'make whole'. Subconsciously, he knows this, which is why he takes off his white coat.

It is important to note that character is not the same as personality. People often confuse the two. It always drove me up the wall when administrators would hire people on the basis of a dynamic personality, that is, on the basis of a good interview, only to discover a few years later what this person is really about, when his or her true character has been revealed. We don't choose our personality; it is determined by a number of factors we have no control over. But character is entirely self-determined, and it is shaped by the free and morally significant choices that we make. Back in 2001,

I was reading a newspaper article about the murder of a priest friend of mine, Monsignor Thomas Wells, and the article made reference to Dr. Stanton Samenow, a forensic psychologist who specializes in the criminal mind. He is one of the few who takes free-choice seriously. Early on in his research, he discovered that prisoners were feeding him answers that they believed he wanted to hear. In other words, he and his partner discovered that they were being played. This led to a paradigm shift; he realized that the Freudianism and Behaviourism in which he was schooled was deficient. Children are not hapless pieces of putty that are shaped and moulded by their environment; rather, they are active agents who shape the environment in which they find themselves. The idea that children are moulded by their environment has caused decent parents a great deal of guilt over the years; they feel responsible for the fact that their child is serving time for serious crimes. But many people who have come from homes with good parents have made the most depraved choices, and there are many who have come from horrible backgrounds and have, nevertheless, made very good choices. Not everyone is a victim of circumstance.

This reminds me of Dr. Murray McGovern, a psychiatrist who would test candidates for the priesthood in the diocese of Hamilton. He did a number of tests on a good priest friend of mine. Candidates would be shown pictures and would be asked to create a story that makes sense out of the scene. My friend created stories that depicted victims of unfortunate circumstances. McGovern warned my friend afterwards that not everyone is a victim; people make choices, and very often they are in difficult situations precisely because of those very choices. If we forget that, we are going to be deceived and taken advantage of. People can and do freely choose evil.

We are building our house here, in this life. What will our house look like? Will it be an ugly, small, dilapidated place where we will live alone for all eternity, because we made ourselves our own god and are simply not drawn to those of opposite character, but repelled? Or will it be a large and unimaginably beautiful house in which the Lord dwells with us for all eternity? So many people today are making the most immoral choices, oblivious to what they are doing to their very own moral identity (character) and the possibility of achieving their destiny (threatening it), all for the sake of temporary goods, such as a good pension and all it will bring, pleasures that will not last because our life here does not last. Whatever moral character we bring with us into eternity, that's what we live with forever, and that character determines who and what we will be attracted to. That is precisely why those who go through life with a conflict of conscience, who are unrepentant of a sin committed at one time, are simply not drawn to the Mass and the practice of the faith. That only continues in eternity. And so, the time of choosing and shaping that dwelling place is now, and if we can't stand to look at ourselves in the mirror of eternity, we will be miserable forever.

The way to beautiful character is to become the person that God intends us to become. If we make choices in accordance with His will, if we are faithful to His commandments—all of them, not most of them—, refusing to compromise our character in the slightest, if we conform our life to the heart of Christ, we will become the beautiful dwelling places we were meant to become. The more we become conformed to him, the more we pray and allow him to shape our character into the person he wants us to be individually and uniquely, the happier we will become, the more beautiful we will become, and the more we will be able to live with ourselves. We can't live with ourselves if Christ is not living with us. Without him, we very subtly begin to despise ourselves, but with him, we see ourselves and others as he sees us, and life becomes far more beautiful.

Christ's life continues in history. His body is historical, and history will achieve the end that God intends for it to achieve. All will be well, as Julian of Norwich so often said. As I mentioned above, it is of the nature of evil to plot, to scheme. Evil is not content to exist in isolation. Think of the tree of the knowledge of good and evil, a symbol of independence from God. The roots are hidden from view, and they spread out in all directions. It is very hard to uproot a tree. It takes a power much greater than that of an individual. Evil grows and spreads. Those who choose to be their own gods are not content to be their own god; they desire to be your god as well, and everyone else's. Evil seeks power. And just as the God of the Old Testament is a jealous God, so too the false gods of this world are jealous gods, and so they plot to destroy their competitor. All evil is essentially conspiratorial.

But evil is difficult to uncover; it is difficult to expose, because it is so brilliantly hidden. It always appears behind a facade of goodness. And we feed evil by choosing not to listen to our intuition when we sense the presence of evil. We want to please, we do not want to disappoint, and so we choose not to disappoint those who belong to evil, but to cooperate with their schemes, all because we so desperately want to please, because when we please others, they are good to us. At the root of the cooperation with evil is a disordered love of the self, a disordered love of one's own life.

But evil has been defeated. Any victories that evil enjoys now are only appearance, just parts of a larger game, and these apparent victories of evil only contribute to the overall beauty of the final product. I remember once following a chess match between Russian chess champion Garry Kasparov and an opponent, and I was astounded at a move that Kasparov made. It appeared to me that he was sacrificing the game. He ended up losing a queen. It made no sense to me. But the sacrifice created the conditions for a victory with pieces of lesser value. It was an astounding game to study; it was beautiful and exhilarating to contemplate. We might be one of those chess pieces that is sacrificed early or later in the game. But if we are on the winning side, we will be part of the victory celebration, and those who chose to play on the wrong side, who chose to sacrifice their integrity for the momentary pleasures of isolated victories, will have nothing in the end; they will not share in the joy of victory, but in the eternal shame of defeat.

Our entire life must become a perpetual prayer. The crosses that we carry are gifts that are very intense and fruitful moments of that prayer. That's how we share in the redemption. That's how we participate in Christ's victory over evil and influence generations to come. Your growth in holiness and charity affects history in ways that you and I simply cannot imagine or conceive. And I believe there is good scientific evidence that lends credence to this point. Some scientists point out that the laws of nature are more like habits than fixed laws. Habits are acquired after repeated activity, so they develop over time, and of course they are hard to break. These habits persist, because there is a memory in nature. But what is interesting is that the habits that things develop influence other things non-locally, things at a distance, across space and in time, so to speak. In other words, once new things have happened and have been repeated, the more often they happen, that is, the more habitual they become. Rupert Sheldrake and physicist David Bohm suggest that this applies to all self-organizing systems: atoms, molecules, crystals, cells, tissues, organs, organisms, societies of organisms, cultures, planets, solar systems, galaxies, etc. At all self-organizing levels there are habits that build up, and there's an inherent memory in nature that enables these habits to be remembered.[2] This can be illustrated by considering the behaviour of crystal formation. It may take months or even years to make a new crystal from a new compound for the first time, because there haven't been any crystals of that specific kind before, but after we have made those crystals, it will be easier to make

---

[2] Rupert Sheldrake. *The Presence of the Past: Morphic Resonance and the Memory of Nature.* Vermont: Park Street Press, 2012. Cf. "Morphic Fields and the Implicate Order: A Dialogue with David Bohm" in Rupert Sheldrake. *Morphic Resonance: The Nature of Formative Causation.* Vermont: Park Street Press, 2009. Appendix B

the same kinds of crystals again, and the more often we do this, the easier it becomes. This phenomenon applies to animal behavior as well. If rats are trained to learn a new trick in London, for example, rats all around the world will learn the same trick more quickly simply because rats have learned it in London. And of course this applies also to human persons; it is getting easier to learn computer programming, skateboarding, windsurfing, and other such skill; there is even an abundance of evidence that this is happening with regard to IQ tests. In the 1980s, very many people were doing IQ tests, and the averages are going up because millions have done IQ tests, not because people are getting smarter. In fact, they've gone up 30% over the course of the 20th century.[3]

This is something that is interesting to study, but I'm going to extend this to the spiritual life. Angels influence one another vertically. What this means is that the angels on the highest level of the hierarchy, the Seraphim, the Cherubim and the Thrones, generously pour out all they've been given to the angels of the

---

[3] *Ibid.*, p. 211.

second hierarchy, the Dominations, Powers and Celestial Virtues, raising them up as far as that is possible. And these angels in turn generously pour out all they've been given, the entire illumination of their minds, to the angels of the lowest hierarchy, raising them up as far as their natures will permit.

But we influence others horizontally. Like everything else in this material universe, when we work to achieve a level of perfection in the spiritual life, a level of holiness, we influence others non-locally, across space and time, in such a way that holiness becomes easier for others. We might be having only a small influence on others locally, but that may not matter in the end. There is something that breaks free of the bounds and limits of locality.[4] You influence the human race by virtue of your achievements. It will be easier for others to grow in wisdom, in charity, in piety, easier for others to forgive and to turn to God in times of darkness, all because you have done so. The human race is mysteriously united across space and time, which is how the inheritance of Original Sin is accounted for.

---

[4] See David Bohm. *Wholeness and the Implicate Order.* New York: Routledge, 2002.

The sin of Adam affected the entire human race, including those who came after him. Christ's death on Good Friday affected the entire human race, before and after him, and we who are a part of his body, our individual acts, our growth in holiness, in charity, in prayer, does not just stay with us. They mysteriously influence others non-locally, across space and time. If that is true of crystals, cells, and animals, how much more for human persons and their spiritual achievements.

We are indebted to so many people who have gone before us. Their choices made it much easier for us to turn to God, to pray, to love, to achieve whatever level of moral integrity we might have achieved. Behind every saint are a myriad of people, for the most part unknown, whose choices, whose devotion, fidelity, whose growth in knowledge, made that saint possible— and these people need not have known the saint in question.

Scripture speaks about this generational influence:

For I, Yahweh your God, am a jealous God and I punish the father's fault in the sons, the grandsons, and the great-grandsons of those who hate me; but I show kindness to

> *thousands of those who love me and keep my*
> *commandments.* (Ex 20, 5ff)

And,

> *For I, the Lord, your God, am a jealous God, bringing*
> *punishment for their parents' wickedness on the children of*
> *those who hate me, down to the third and fourth generation,*
> *but showing love down to the thousandth generation of those*
> *who love me and keep my commandments. (Dt 5, 9-10)*

Of course, these verses must be carefully interpreted—
for they are easily misinterpreted. What these words
point to, I believe, is the influence sin has on posterity,
and the greater influence holiness has on posterity. That
there is scientific corroboration for this is quite
fascinating. Just as we are indebted to a myriad of
others who are unknown to us, there are a myriad of
others who will be indebted to us.

Your hidden acts of faith, hope, and charity, your
hidden prayer life, is effective in ways we are unaware
of. But this horizontal influence does not proceed in
one direction only (i.e., forward); it may also move
backward into the past by virtue of non-locality. The
reason this is possible is that God is not subject to the
limits of space and time, and so, although we pray at a

particular place within a particular time, we pray to God
who is not subject to those limits (of place and time),
and so it follows that as a result of our intercession, He
can choose to create the conditions for the fulfilment of
our prayers at any point in time, conditions that exist
before we even utter those prayers, but which exist by
virtue of those prayers. In other words, our prayers
affect the past as well as the present—which implies
that it is never too late to pray.

One of the most important acts that influence
others non-locally is forgiveness. Forgiveness is so
important that we cannot enter eternity without
forgiving all those in our lives whom we need to
forgive. Which reminds me of a story involving my
mother. She was born in 1928, in Nice, France, one
year before the arrival of the Great Depression. When
he was 15 years old, my great grandfather hopped a
freight train from New Jersey to New York and found a
job in a stenographer's office. He worked hard and
eventually made his way all the way up to becoming
vice-president of the New York telephone company.
His son, my grandfather, Walter Cahill, was studying
law at Princeton when his father died. Knowing at that

point that he wouldn't ever have to work a day in his life, he chose to leave Princeton and moved to Nice, where he lived a rather Epicurean lifestyle and became known for throwing great parties for his friends, the likes of which included Ernst Hemingway, F. Scott Fitzgerald, William Somerset Maugham, Pablo Picasso, and playwright Eugene O'Neill, to whom he was closest.

My mother had two sisters who were teenagers when she was born and whom she never knew growing up. At the age of four, after spending the summer with her mother in Portage, Quebec, my mother was left to begin school in a convent in Riviere-du-Loup, Quebec, while her mother, by then divorced, went off to live in New York City. There was no abuse at the convent, but the atmosphere was neither light nor kind. Every spring her mother would return from New York and they would spend the summer in Portage. By this time my mother's sisters would have been finished school in England and France. Josephine, my mother's oldest sister, was fifteen years her senior and grew up in a boarding school in England, while Dorothy, thirteen years her senior, went to a boarding school in France.

Why were they separated so far from one another? My mother explained it this way: my grandparents were not meant for parenthood, she'd say. They traveled, and when one of their children reached school age (4 years), they would be left at the boarding school in the country where they happen to have been visiting (England, France, or Quebec), and that is where their daughter would spend her childhood and adolescent years. Christmas and Easter were spent in the lonely solitude of the convent, at least in my mother's case.

Shortly thereafter my mother went to the Ursuline nuns in Quebec City, a convent also thin on kindness and a touch heavy on gloom, and where students were almost as cloistered as the nuns. Only one nun, she recalls, showed her any kindness at all, an American nun, Sister Aloysius.

They'd sleep in dormitories; for only the older students had their own rooms. She was not allowed out of the convent, except on one or two Sundays a year; friends could come to take them out. My mother recalls a few times going to a friend's for Sunday dinner.

She would spend her summers with her mother in a hotel in Portage, an old place with a long and wide verandah that encircled the entire house. In later years they'd rent a house from a farmer who had eighteen children who lived in the back of the house they rented. At the convent my mother would daydream. All she dreamed about was to have a family and raise children like everybody else. She was at the convent until she was sixteen years of age; my grandfather had come to see her and spoke to her behind a grid, and she said to him then that she wanted to leave. She said to me that her own father was a stranger to her at that point. It was only after leaving that my mother first met her sister, Josephine, a warm and caring woman in whom my mother discovered a mother that she'd never really had.

My mother describes my grandmother's life as tragic. She was bright, well read, and could have done something with her life; for she always had an income, but never worked a day in her life. In later years my grandmother would occasionally be overcome by feelings of guilt; she'd cry, lamenting that her daughter had such an awful upbringing.

It was never easy for my mother to talk of these days. I thought there might come a time when I'd want to write about her life, and so when she came to live with us, I'd try to persuade her to reminisce out loud while I took notes. These sessions, though, never did last very long. After about ten minutes she'd become noticeably irritated and I'd have to stop.

When my mother died, she was twenty years sober. She had begun to drink heavily about a year or so before I went off to university. I was given the task of sitting down with her one spring day to tell her that she had a drinking problem. She appeared to be open to what I had to say and readily agreed to seek out Alcoholics Anonymous. It was only years later that she told me she felt like hitting me over the head with her cast iron frying pan for daring to suggest she was an alcoholic. But that year marked the beginning of a new life for her.

My mother eventually ended up working as an addiction counselor for Street Haven at the Crossroads in Toronto. I couldn't formulate all that I've learned from her over the years, some of which include the importance of trusting in Divine Providence, and the importance of gratitude, and kindness, especially towards those who suffer. And we had many great moments that I hope will never take leave of my memory, such as the times I'd read to her from the writings of Maugham, Steinbeck, and O'Neill. The Danforth in Toronto holds some of the most recent memories. It was there, in one of the Greek restaurants that line the street, that we began talking about the Ursuline nuns.

"Do you think you can forgive the nuns for their lack of kindness?" I asked her one day.

"Oh, sure," was her reply, which was immediately followed by a retraction:

"Well, no. I won't. Why should I?"

I didn't expect such a retraction. I was surprised. We moved on to discuss other things, but I'd always kept this "unforgiveness" in the back of my mind.

During the Christmas holidays of 2000 while visiting one of my sisters, my mother fell and broke her hip. She was not recovering well in the new year. One night during the March Break of 2001, she'd suffered six seizures and fell into a coma. After coming out of the coma—which surprised us all—, she lived with a relatively severe case of dementia. Her dementia, however, was in some ways a great blessing. She didn't fully understand what was happening to her, and she could not remember "yesterdays", so every day was entirely new. Some days she'd recognize me, other days I was my deceased brother, and sometimes I was, in her vague memory of yesterday, a young priest who dropped by to visit.

At the beginning of the summer, on the second or third day after her arrival, I sat with her in the wing of the nursing home that was just minutes away my home. I was trying to think of things to talk about. Suddenly she spoke up: "A priest came this morning to say Mass. It was very nice."

I wasn't sure whether she dreamed this or whether it was real. I tried to imagine where our local pastor would set up to say Mass on a Tuesday morning in such a small nursing home. Gazing out into space, she said: "He spoke of forgiveness."

I thought about this for a moment, then asked her: "If you were to think of one person in your life that you need to forgive, who would it be?"

She thought for a few seconds and said, "I don't know."

"You don't know?"

"I don't know."

So, I thought for a moment and recalled a picture of my mother when she was four years old, dressed in a black tunic, ready to be sent off to the convent in Riviere-du-Loup. "Maybe your mother?"

"My mother?" she said. "Yes, maybe my mother. Yes, my mother."

After a minute or two, I got an idea: "Mom, let's try something. Close your eyes."

She closed her eyes.

"Imagine your mother."

She followed carefully.

"Now say out loud, "Mother, I forgive you."

I watched her face for about half a minute, not sure whether she was awake or asleep. Finally, she moved herself to a more comfortable position on the wheelchair and said: "No, I don't think so."

I was stunned. Of course she can't forgive her mother at this time. She was abandoned. I've never been abandoned, and so I have no idea what it must be like to live seventy years with painful memories of abandonment. Did I really think that a simple exercise in the corridor of a small nursing home was going to heal years of dark and sorrowful memories? But I knew then what my work was for the summer. She was not ready to die; my work was to help get her get ready for death, that is, to help her through the healing process towards forgiveness, and her dementia is just what I needed to succeed.

God's providence is marvelous. It is ingenious; for I never would have been able to get away with this had she not had dementia. So, I returned the following day, brought her to the same spot, sat down on the rocking chair, and we talked. After a while I began:

"I heard there was a Mass here yesterday"

"Was there?"

"Yes. And I heard the priest spoke about forgiveness."

"Oh, did he?"

"Hey, mom, let me ask you, if you were to think of someone in your life that you need to forgive, who would it be?"

There was no hesitating this time around. Immediately she replied: "Oh, I'd have to say my mother."

"Really?"

"Definitely my mother."

"Hey, mom, why don't we try something. Close your eyes."

She closed her eyes.

"Imagine your mother."

"Oh, my!" she said. "She's right there."

"She's right there?"

"I see her so clearly."

"Why don't you tell her how angry you are for abandoning you when you were four."

She hesitated.

"You have a right to be angry," I said to her. "No one should ever abandon their child if they have the means of raising her. Tell her how angry you are."

And so she did, speaking with great emotion, and telling her how mean it was to leave her in a foreign country for so many years, only to see her once each year for a summer vacation on the beach.

I began to wonder whether I was a little out of my element here. How am I going to bring her back out of this anger? I thought to myself. But I managed to do so, and eventually brought her back to her room. She'd wrap her arms around my neck, and I'd lift her up out of her wheelchair and into her bed. The following day I read from the same script: "Let me ask you, mom, if you were to think of one person in your life that you need to forgive, who would it be?"

I continued this for a number of days, allowing her to spend some of her anger. And much to my own dismay, I even spoke on behalf of my grandmother. Eventually my mother was able to say what she was unable to say weeks earlier: "I forgive you, mother." Doing so brought about a noticeable change in her. She seemed much lighter the following day.

But a sadness came over me one night as I left for the parking lot. Her work was done. She has forgiven her mother. What more is there for her to do? There's no reason for her to stay around. I knew that it wasn't long before she'd be going home. When the phone rang the following Saturday morning and displayed the name of the nursing home, I knew that this was the beginning of the end. She died two weeks later and was buried on the morning of September 11, 2001.

I am grateful that God that He did not allow my mother to die without the opportunity to forgive her own mother; for it is not possible to enter into eternal life without learning to forgive everyone we need to forgive (Mt 6, 14-15; Mk 11, 25-26); for no person will allow himself to receive God's unlimited forgiveness unless he himself has chosen to forgive everyone in his past: "The amount you measure out will be the amount you receive" (Mt 7, 2). No one will allow himself any more than what he has measured out, and so from this perspective, there is a fundamental justice that no one will allow him or herself to violate. Sin creates a debt that exceeds an individual person's ability to satisfy. To be forgiven, the human person requires a forgiveness that has no limits, for sin against God creates a debt we cannot satisfy. The person who harbors unforgiveness against another, who places a limit on what he chooses to forgive, renders himself unable to receive the divine forgiveness, which has no limits. To forgive is to 'give afore', to consent to give the offender his offense against you. It is an acceptance of the suffering we previously underwent as a result of his offense against us. Our redemption is precisely an act of forgiveness, it is Christ's acceptance of the suffering caused by sin. All forgiveness is thus an entering into this act of redemption.

This life has a lot to do with learning to put up with one another. It has everything to do with learning to forgive one another. Whenever I come across a student who is difficult to put up with, my memory rarely fails to bring forth images of myself at a certain point in my history. In this way I am reminded of the people who had to learn to put up with me. I then realize the debt I owe them and that the opportunity to put up with this rather obnoxious student now is precisely the opportunity given to me at this moment of paying that debt. The more students like these that I encounter, the more I am forced to recall the debt I owe to friends, parents, siblings, teachers, mentors, and colleagues. If we learn this difficult work of forgiveness, we've done our work, and, for some of us at least, there may not be anything left for us to do. Only then are we able to open ourselves up to receive the unlimited breadth and depth of God's forgiveness of our own sins against Him.

3434333333

Divine Comedy and the Mystery of the Cross

Jesus defeated the evil one in the desert, and it is because of that victory that each one of us has the capacity to rise above each of these temptations in order to achieve our salvation. But there is one battle left, and this battle bears upon the mystery of suffering and death. Life is full of suffering, and there is no getting around that. Moreover, each life ends in death, from which everyone recoils. The most basic fear is the fear of death.

These points are at the heart of the religion of Buddhism. Siddhartha Gautama, who lived 2,500 years ago, was desperate to find an answer to the mystery of suffering. His father shielded him from suffering, never let him leave the palace boundaries, provided him with every comfort, but the story speaks of the Great Going Forth. Siddhartha insists on leaving, so his father instructs his servants to shield him from the specter of death and anything associated with it, such as poverty and suffering. But his plan fails; Siddhartha sees what his father tried to shield him from, and the result is a

107

determination to solve the problem of human suffering. He is moved to join some Hindu aesthetics to live a life of extreme renunciation, but he eventually discovers the middle way and formulates the fundamental teaching of the four noble truths: all is suffering, the root of suffering is disordered desire, the solution to suffering is to drop all desire, and the path to enlightenment is the noble eightfold path.

There is tremendous wisdom in Buddhism, as there is in all of the great religions of the world. But I bring up Buddhism only because it really does arise out of the question of the mystery of suffering. And so too the life of Christ cannot be understood except in light of the mystery of human suffering and death. There is, however, a radical difference—and this difference does not cancel Buddhism; it actually complements it in many ways. Christ did not come to bring an end to suffering, nor to offer a solution to it as though it were a problem with a solution. Rather, the Second Person of the Trinity joined a human nature to himself in order to enter into human suffering and to join his divine life to his own death. Christ came to transform human suffering and death.

We cannot escape suffering; it is simply not possible; and we cannot escape death. Every day that passes is one day closer to the grave. But each one of us clings to life; we want to live forever. Not necessarily in this state, but we want a happiness that is enduring, that does not come to an end, and so if we want a happiness that does not come to an end, we want a life that does not come to an end. But death contradicts this desire, for it is the end of everything we have achieved. And yet, facing death with faith turns out to be a very positive experience. I remember when I drove a Ford, my first car was an 88 Mustang. After a few years, I began spending lots of time at Nick's Garage on Weston Rd. He was a great mechanic, always about two thirds cheaper than any other place that fixes cars. He also had a crucifix in his office. But the problem was you had to wait, sometimes for hours. But it was worth the wait. What I would often do in the meantime is go for a walk around the neighborhood, and at the end of the street that was just south of his garage was St. John's Cemetery on the Humber. At the time I was teaching in the Jane and Finch area of Toronto, and those first 10 years were very stressful—it was a terribly broken neighborhood and teaching there was not easy. I remember one stressful day walking through that cemetery reading the tombstones while my car was being looked at. I'd calculate how long this person buried here lived, and I'd do the same for the next one, and so on. Then the thought occurred to me: "That person had the same stresses and worries that I have now and look where he is. What good did worry do him?" And I'd keep that thought for the next tombstone, aware that perhaps I'll be there soon enough. So why am I carrying all this worry? The result was quite remarkable: a weight was lifted off my shoulders; I felt much lighter. It is when we remember our own death and keep it at the forefront of our minds that we begin to live more fully in the present moment.

It's a strange paradox, because death contradicts our deepest desires; it marks the end of everything we yearn for. It is the dissolution and disintegration of the human person and our greatest fear. But the eternal Logos, the Second Person of the Trinity, God Himself, joined a human nature to Himself in order to change our death; not to take it away, but to make death life giving. He came to inject death with his own divine life.

As a result of that decision, death is no longer the final word of despair and loneliness. Rather, each person can now find another Person at the very heart of his own death, and that other Person is the Person of the Son, the Second Person of the Trinity. Death becomes an experience of eternal life. He came to enter into human suffering, so that when we suffer, we don't suffer alone, but can find the life we yearn for at the heart of that suffering.

Suffering can now shape us into a likeness to Christ. Had the Second Person of the Trinity chosen not to enter into human suffering, then it would have remained meaningless, entirely negative, a signal that our life is disintegrating. It would render our lives hopelessly ugly, and we'd have no choice but to use every ounce of energy to evade it. But Christ entered into it. Beauty Itself entered into the ugliness of human suffering, so that all those who suffer with Him can now become like him, more conformed to him, beautified in him. Christ gratuitously gives to each suffering person a power and dignity that is his or hers to receive or reject; for this life is about becoming Christ, it is about decreasing so that he may increase in

us, as St. John the Baptist said: "He must increase, I
must decrease" (Jn 3, 30). St. Paul said: "It is no longer
I who live, but Christ lives in me" (Gal 2, 20). Our
purpose is to become Christ, and our relationship to
suffering is now the way of becoming him.

Death is our final act. Death is humiliating, for we
are deprived of all power. The illusion of independence
is over, the illusion of control has been shattered. Death
disillusions each one of us. It reveals our true status: we
are from the earth, *humus,* and our relationship to death
measures the extent of our humanness. This final
turning towards the soil can now be our final prayer: a
final offering to God, an offering of our entire person
along with everything we have achieved and not
achieved, as well as our failures. There is a sense in
which death is the ultimate failure, but now His divine
life can be discovered there. The reason is that the
Second Person of the Trinity is eternal. In joining a
human nature, He enters into time. The eternal is joined
to time, that is, to each moment of time. Quoting
Vatican II, St. John Paul II pointed out, "by his
Incarnation, he, the Son of God, in a certain way,
united himself with each man" (*Redemptor Hominis*, 13).

He is intimately united to every human person, and each one of us, on a very profound level, is intimately united to every man. But when the Word, the very heart of the Trinity, joins a human nature, the eternal is intimately present to each moment of time. He tasted death, and in doing so he injected it with his life, so that death can be a beautiful and life-giving experience, without it ceasing to be a difficult experience. We don't die alone, and we no longer die in despair. Death is no longer the final word of defeat and loss; rather, it is the final act of a life of prayer.

That's how powerful God is. He is so powerful that He can allow Himself to be murdered, and not even that destroys Him. He gives life to everything He touches, and He has touched the death of every man.

Death Transformed into Comedy

In touching death, however, the Word transforms tragedy into comedy. It is possible now to take death lightly. And the saints do just that; they take themselves very lightly; a spirit of humor permeates their lives, a spirit that enables them to rise above their own suffering and death. This is evident in the lives of the martyrs, who would often joke about themselves on their way to execution. William Roper tells of his father in law, Thomas More, who joked with the Master Lieutenant as he was being escorted up a weak scaffold: "I pray you, Master Lieutenant, see me safe up, and for my coming down let me shift for myself". With a cheerful countenance, he said to the executioner: "Pluck up thy spirits, man, and be not afraid to do thine office; my neck is very short; take heed therefore thou strike not awry, for saving of thine honesty."

And yet Thomas wrote some of his best theological works while imprisoned in the Tower, evidently more concerned for the truth of Christ and the souls outside the Tower than for his own life. Although they take their own lives and deaths lightly, they take the souls of others very seriously; that is why they take the moral law very seriously, because the moral choices we make have great weight. Our moral choices dispose us in a certain way; they dispose us to receive an increase in divine grace, or they dispose us to turn away from the invitation to eternal life. The psychopath, on the other hand, takes himself very seriously, but takes the lives of others very lightly. That is why the psychopath takes sex lightly; it has little significance for him because the lives of others, especially those he uses sexually, have very little significance.

Those who dwell in darkness don't mind playing with people, using them, manipulating them like pawns in their own little game that has as its end the maximum level of glorification that they can procure for themselves. Such people do not have the eyes to laugh at themselves, for they never see any incongruity between themselves and a higher law or standard that measures them, because they refuse to acknowledge and submit to any law other than their own will.

A person has to affirm a law greater, a law more beautiful than his own will, in order to be able to laugh at himself, as he beholds how much he has fallen short of the standard it holds out to him. Instead, the egoist laughs at others whom he takes lightly, and he does so sardonically.

Laughter is a mysterious phenomenon. A key to unlocking the mystery of humor in order to explore it more deeply is the word itself, again from the Latin *humus*, which means 'soil', 'dirt', or 'ground'. The word 'humility' is also derived from the Latin *humus*. A humble person is one who has not forgotten his origins, namely, his origin in God: "…the Lord God…breathed into his nostrils the breath of life; and the man became a living being" (Gn 2, 7); as well as his origin 'from the ground': "Let me take it upon myself to speak to the Lord, I who am but dust and ashes" (Gn 18, 27). The humble man, among other things, knows he is smaller than God, entirely dependent upon him, and subject to his law, and he knows that he is weak and vulnerable to destruction like any other material thing. Moreover, he refuses to ascend to heights disproportionate to his material nature, unlike the proud man who stubbornly insists on being his own god and the measure of what is true and good; the proud have very little sense of their own limitations. Humility is akin to humor because the more humble a person is, the more a spirit of humor permeates his life, and thus the more he is able to laugh, in particular at himself. Evil has a narcissistic or egotistical character to it, and one quality that egoists lack is the ability to laugh at themselves.

To be human is to exist at this juncture between God above and the ground below, and it is only here, suspended between heaven and earth, that genuine humor is at all possible. A person who is far too immersed in the affairs of the earth, and who loves the earth inordinately, laughs with great difficulty. He is too serious, and his mind is far too weighed down by the matter of the world to see himself and others from a distance and against the background of the divine law, which is the angle from which joyful laughter is made possible.

A person who is so elevated off the ground laughs with great difficulty as well, because he has forgotten that he is from the earth (dirt, soil). He is no longer aware of his fumbling nature, his limitations, and so he lives under the illusion that he is in control—and how can he laugh when he will no longer be surprised.

Humor exists in that space between heaven and earth in which one beholds the affairs of fallible, fumbling, forgetful human persons in light of the divine law. That is why the saints exhibit the greatest sense of humor. Consider the humor in irony. The nicknames that children give to one another are often very funny, because they are full of irony. Think of Hercules, the kid so named because he couldn't lift a sack of potatoes to save his life, or the tall kid whose friends call Shorty, or the short kid they call Stretch, and the fat kid called 'Slim'. Or, think of the child that laughs at the TV when a witch turns a man into a frog, or the proud man who walks high and mighty, then suddenly slips on a banana peel, or bends over to pick up the newspaper and rips his pants at the seat. We laugh because we are struck by the irony, the latter a kind of reparative irony, that is, a much-needed reminder that we are only matter and spirit.

When we consider these two aspects of humor, namely humility and irony, we see that God really has a great sense of humor. The Incarnation of the Son of God is a perfect blend of irony and humility. St. Gregory of Nyssa highlights the irony in the Incarnation in his *Sermons on the Beatitudes*:

> What more humble for the King of creation than to share in our poor nature? The Ruler of rulers, the Lord of lords puts on voluntarily the garb of servitude. The Judge of all things becomes a subject of governors; He who holds the universe in His hands finds no place in the inn, but is cast

aside into the manger of irrational beasts. The perfectly Pure accepts the filth of human nature, and after going through all our poverty passes on to the experience of death. Look at the standard by which to measure voluntary poverty! Life tastes death; the Judge is brought to judgment, the Lord of the life of all creatures is sentenced by the judge; the King of all heavenly powers does not push aside the hands of the executioners. Take this, He says, as an example by which to measure your humility.

Furthermore, God, who cannot be contained, but who contains all, chooses to remain really and truly present to us under the appearance of ordinary bread. Imagine if one were to hold up a piece of rye bread and declare out loud: "This is my uncle Joe. He promised that he would remain present to the family after his death, in this piece of bread". Turning to the rye bread he continues: "We miss you, uncle Joe. We love you! You'll always be close by, in the bread basket, and we'll greet you daily on one knee."

We'd be compelled to laugh at such a spectacle, for it is ridiculous. But God the Son has chosen to do just that, to remain substantially present to us under the appearance of ordinary and unexciting bread. The sense of ridicule is gone, because love is serious, and above all, it is true, Christ is the Bread of Life, literally. But the humor is still mystically discernible; for here is humility and irony at its best; for it is divine humor, and the joke is on those who do not believe it and who ridicule those who do. The Eucharist is the perfect example of the humility that takes itself lightly.

The Incarnation reveals not only the absolute mercy of God, but it reveals at the same time the joyful humor of God. When we enter into the life of the Trinity by faith, we enter into God's humor. I often stop at a Greek Orthodox Church on the way home from work to behold the icons. There is a very large icon there of St. John the Baptist holding his head in his hands. That is tragedy turned to comedy. There is something genuinely humorous about that icon; the tragedy has been transcended by the joy and hope of eternal life. We can laugh because death is not the final word, rather, humor has the last laugh in this case.

I recall the reaction of a very gifted but quiet student of mine upon coming to understand some very profound truths on the soul, universals and the nature of knowledge in the thought of Plato. On more than one occasion, I'd look over in his direction to find him laughing by himself. I finally inquired of his laughter, and he simply pointed out: "I get it". He came to understand. Truth is beautiful, it is awe inspiring, and in his case he was moved to joyous laughter as some of the loftiest ideas of Plato came in contact with a spirit that is united to matter. The joy and surprise of coming into the possession of what is eternally true spilled over into his body, inducing him to laugh.

And God is Truth Itself. He is subsistent Truth, just as He is subsistent Being, Goodness, and Beauty. To behold God as He is in Himself is to be possessed by Joy Itself, and a body possessed by Joy is one that is disposed to laughter.

This is different from the person for whom everything is a joke, for whom everything is to be taken lightly. They take everyone lightly; even the souls of others they take lightly, because they take sin lightly— something the saint will never do, because "blessed are those who mourn" is one of the psychological contours of his mind and heart. He mourns the sins of the world; but it is a hopeful mourning, a joyful one. There is no mourning in the life of the buffoon who has convinced himself that it is well to take the lives of others lightly;

he is light of heart because he is light of mind; he is without the mind of Christ.

Divine Playfulness

Not only is the mystery of humor rooted in the mystery of God; so too the mystery of play. Comedy is a type of playing. A good comedian plays with his audience. He depends, however, on an audience that is willing to play along.

Creation as well as the re-creation of our redemption, is divine play; it is a sacred game. Even for us, recreation typically involves play. To play—because it is a type of leisure—is to engage in activity not for the sake of some further end, but simply for its own sake. It is activity that is meaningful in itself. Human play involves a space in which to play, a field, and the game to be played will have an intelligible structure, with rules, boundaries, penalties for infractions, and goals. It will involve a physical and/or mental struggle to achieve the goal; one that brings rest, even when it is strenuous, for it is a leisurely and intriguing struggle.

The game—if it involves teams—aims principally at a common good, to be shared in whole and entire by every player, namely victory. But once play begins, the game cannot be controlled as a whole, but acquires a life of its own that is larger than any one individual. It is always full of surprises, which is why it is so much fun. The players become part of a kind of mini providence, a field of influence, without which there can be no fun, and thus no game.

For this reason, to control the game, such as its outcome, is to allow it to lose its hold on us, and this would drain it of its meaning. A game controlled by any one or more individuals is not a game as those playing might believe it is. Rather, it is a sham, not a playing between equals. In such a situation, the players have been lied to, they are reduced to pawns to serve the personal or private ends of a manipulator. So too is the audience being played. In other words, the childlike quality of the players and spectators—the quality which makes play possible—is being exploited.

Genuine play begets narrative. It is contemplative. Human persons will discuss a good play that is part of a larger game for years afterwards. Baseball's most eloquent and illustrious poet and former Commissioner, Bartlett Giomatti, writes:

> ...the fullest, most expansive, most public talk is the talk in the lobby, baseball's second-favorite venue. The lobby is the park of talk; it is the enclosed place where the game is truly told, because told again and again. Each time it is played and replayed in the telling, the fable is refined, the nuances burnished the color of old silver. The memories in baseball become sharpest as they recede, for the art of telling improves with age.[5]

Play inspires narrative because like a powerful current, the game sweeps the observer off his feet, elevating him to a new level of participation and observation (contemplation). It is restful for both player and observer, because the game takes us out of the workaday world and into a higher order in which one is no longer conscious of the world's time that closes us in and hurries us on, but a heavenly time that does not limit, but liberates. This is especially evident in baseball,

---

[5] *A Great and Glorious Game*. New York: Algonquin Books, 1997, p. 111.

where there is no clock. The game itself has become the clock.

That is why a game, even a playing season, anticipates eternity. Bartlett Giomatti writes:

> Mutability had turned the seasons and translated hope to memory once again. And, once again, she had used baseball, our best invention to stay change, to bring change on. That is why it breaks my heart, that game—not because in New York they could win because Boston lost; in that, there is a rough justice, a reminder to the Yankees of how slight and fragile are the circumstances that exalt one group of human beings over another. It breaks my heart because it was meant to, because it was meant to foster in me again the illusion that there was something abiding, some pattern and some impulse that could come together to make a reality that would resist the corrosion; and because, after it had fostered again that most hungered-for illusion, the game was meant to stop, and betray precisely what it promised....I need to think something lasts forever, and it might as well be that state of being that is a game; it might as well be that, in a green field, in the sun.[6]

---

[6] *Ibid.*, pp.12-13.

The Wisdom of God, who is with God and who is God (Jn 1, 1), eternally plays before the face of God like a child: "When he established the heavens, I was there,…when he marked out the foundations of the earth, then I was beside him, like a little child; and I was daily his delight, making play before him always, at play in his inhabited world and delighting in the sons of men" (Prov 8, 27, 29-31). *Chokmah* can be translated as wit, skillful, wisely, or wisdom. The Wisdom that 'makes play' before God is witty, wise, skillful. He is like a child, because children play. At the same time, He is like an artist who plays wittily and skillfully.

God creates through the *Logos*, His Word, who plays. In other words, God's creating is a divine playing, and creation is His divine game. Divine providence is the rhythm of that game, which exists for us who are both players and spectators in one. Creation does not proceed from God out of necessity, but out of a love that freely chooses to communicate itself and make itself visible. As the artist creates on the basis of what he sees, similarly God, who knows Himself in His Word who is Wisdom Itself, playing like a child before Him, creates according to what He sees in His Word.

And so, creation reflects marvelously and of course imperfectly and in varied ways the beauty and wit of this divine playfulness of the *Logos*. To contemplate the works of the Word is to be drawn into his playing, and so it should come as no surprise that we are moved to play wittily and creatively. To behold the beauty of this world is often to be inspired to express it and imitate it in some limited way, either in song, dance, prose or verse, or on canvas, or else to enter into the beautiful works of others.

Children know naturally how to play, and they are very serious about their play. Try disrupting the play of children—i.e., take the ball and run—and we soon discover that the playful is not opposed to the serious. And children are very serious about law; for they understand that law is an integral part of play. As they gather friends to play, they immediately go about drawing boundary lines, promulgating the law, the rules, the penalties for infraction; for without law there is no playing. Law exists to make play a possibility, that is, for the sake of the freedom to play. It is ordered, intelligible, harmonious, and protective of the good, in this case, the good of the game. One cannot arbitrarily decide, after hitting the ball, to run to third then back home again; rather, one must proceed to first base, then second, third, then home. The kid who refuses to play by the rules is not serious enough about the game. He ruins the fun for everyone.

Only those who want to play by their own rules, those who want to control the outcome of the game, see law as restrictive, burdensome, and opposed to liberty. Those who refuse to play because it isn't their game see in law a desire to dominate and control, but only because they cannot imagine the possibility that others might be radically different from themselves and are willing to submit to a higher law for the sake of being taken up into the field—like a magnetic field— that orders the parts, taking them up into the joy of the game.

Man's destiny is to learn to play the Lord's game, which is a very specific game with rules, some of which are absolute, and some relative. We are invited to enter into this divine game so as to enter into the Sabbath rest of His divine and eternal playing. To learn to play is to learn to become a child again: "Truly I tell you, unless you change and become like children, you will never enter the kingdom of heaven" (Mt 18, 3). For what is it that children love to do above all things? They love to play. Without play, there is no childhood, and without a childhood, one does not know how to be an adult.

How does one play? By surrendering to divine providence, that is, by allowing oneself to be taken up into the Lord's re-creation; it is to enter into the game of grace, the Person of Christ, who descended in order to lift us up into the humor and play of the Divine Persons. His game is profoundly serious, and it is bound by strict rules and foul lines. But those rules and foul lines exist for the sake of the beauty and order of the play, not to mention the good of the players.

The point of this game, like baseball, is to return home. Some of us may be called to make a sacrifice fly so that the man on third can make it home, but all of us are called ultimately to help one another home, and when the enemy takes an aggressive posture, all of us must play our positions faithfully, patiently, without changing the rules that are not ours to change.

It is possible, however, to lose our balance in a number of ways. Like those who refuse to play, we can, even while belonging to the right team, begin to take ourselves too seriously and the souls of others too lightly. In this case, our spirit of playfulness is not genuine; it is self-deception; a false joy, a disordered love of pleasure. We end up compromising with the world, because we love our life in the world too much, that is, we love the goods of this world too much. Some become bored with childhood and delight in seeing themselves as slightly larger (inflated) than they actually are—the elite who see themselves as smarter than everyone else. They become micromanagers; for being an individual member of a large team is not all that flattering, and that is why some will experiment in ways that exceed the boundaries of the game. Inevitably, they will hide their recklessness under the guise of being light of heart. The problem is that they fail to take seriously enough what pertains to the salvation of souls. Another way to lose one's balance involves a heavy spirit. These are serious about souls, but they as well are too serious about themselves. They lack an awareness of the limitations and constraints that sense perception, geography and time impose on human knowing. They have become dogmatic, self-righteous, clerical even, suspicious of those with whom they do not see eye to eye. And they fail to grasp the character of the game of which they are a part, that games are not, as a whole, controlled by coaches, managers, or team captains, but have a life of their own. These people are not secure in God, and so they laugh rarely.

But if we don't join this game, inevitably we join another, the game of those opposed to providence, one fast paced, unfestive, strenuous and exhausting, one in which to play is to work, ultimately for nothing. Behind this game is an empty promise of rest, and the humor that belongs to it is derisive and mocking, one that plays with reputations, soils the character, perverts the order of things, and aims to expose what it sees as the façade of moral nobility.

When the playing becomes difficult, when it rains and we are losing, we need only remember that a game is meant to be played in a spirit of joy. For we have an advantage in that we've been told and have been asked to believe that victory is guaranteed, not our own individual victory—unless we persevere—, but the victory of the team. It is right to taste the sadness of losing an inning, but we despair if we forget that the game is ours and we have a part to play in this larger victory.

Deacon Douglas McManaman was born in Toronto and grew up in Montreal. He studied philosophy at the University of St. Jerome's College (Waterloo) and theology at the University of Montreal. He is a permanent deacon of the Archdiocese of Toronto and ministers to those with mental illness. He currently teaches philosophy and the Theory of Knowledge at Father Michael McGivney Catholic Academy in Markham, Ontario and is chaplain of the Toronto Chapter of the Catholic Teachers Guild. He is a regular contributor to Lifeissues.net and his recent books include *The Logic of Anger* (Justin Press, 2015), and *Christ Lives!* (Justin Press, 2017), as well as *The Morally Beautiful*, *Introduction to Philosophy for Young People*, *Readings in the Theory of Knowledge*, *Basic Catholicism*, and *A Treatise on the Four Cardinal Virtues*. He has two podcast channels: *Podcasts for the Religious*, and *Podcasts for Young Philosophers*. He currently lives with his wife and daughter in Aurora, Ontario, Canada.